Contents

Porsche

Ferdinand (Ferry) Porsche   Ferdinand Alexander (Butzi) Porsche   Ferdinand Karl (Burli) Piëch

Foreword by F. A. Porsche

Enthusiasm for the car, a love of engineering and the urge to express these in a pleasing form – this is the combination that provided the creative stimulus for my grandfather and has done for our family ever since. While his first cars could still be described as motorised carriages, reflecting both his own origins and the craft-based approach to vehicle manufacture at the time, he nevertheless sought and, through engineering, soon arrived at the supremely functional form of the motor car in its own right.

From the design of the basic utility car our family progressed logically to the development of sports and racing cars, the principal function of which is safely to attain higher speeds. Our history from the beginning of the century to the present day clearly testifies to the consistent manner in which Porsche has continued its work on this synthesis. For me, in all modesty, it provides conclusive proof of the truth of the old saying that a perfect instrument is a thing of beauty because its form follows its function. This idea has indeed always been our inspiration.

For this exhibition the Design Museum has intuitively and unerringly selected the most significant Porsche developments in both form and engineering. We are delighted at this, especially since cars so rarely feature as the subject of design exhibitions, despite the fact that, after architecture, the car as 'utility sculpture' has come to characterise our sense of form and our image of our cities and streets more than any other object in the twentieth century.

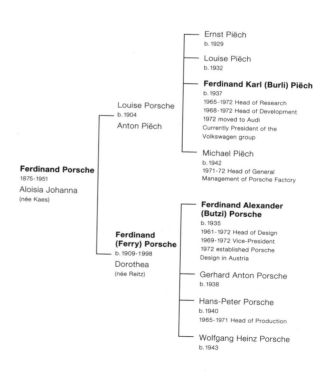

Ferdinand Porsche
1875-1951
Aloisia Johanna
(née Kaes)

Louise Porsche
b. 1904
Anton Piëch

Ernst Piëch
b. 1929

Louise Piëch
b. 1932

Ferdinand Karl (Burli) Piëch
b. 1937
1965-1972 Head of Research
1968-1972 Head of Development
1972 moved to Audi
Currently President of the
Volkswagen group

Michael Piëch
b. 1942
1971-72 Head of General
Management of Porsche Factory

Ferdinand (Ferry) Porsche
b. 1909-1998
Dorothea
(née Reitz)

**Ferdinand Alexander
(Butzi) Porsche**
b. 1935
1961-1972 Head of Design
1969-1972 Vice-President
1972 established Porsche
Design in Austria

Gerhard Anton Porsche
b. 1938

Hans-Peter Porsche
b. 1940
1965-1971 Head of Production

Wolfgang Heinz Porsche
b. 1943

Ferdinand

Design Dynasty 1900–1998

Introduction by Paul Frère

On 8 June 1998, midway through the Design Museum's exhibition, the Porsche company celebrates the fiftieth anniversary of the production of its first car. But the Porsche family name has been central to the history of the automobile for the whole of the twentieth century. The Porsche dynasty comprises three generations of designer-engineers: Ferdinand Porsche (1875-1951), his son Ferry (b.1909-1998), Ferry's son Butzi (b.1935) and nephew Ferdinand Piëch (b.1937). Ferdinand Porsche was above all an engineer, but one whose contribution to automotive design remains unparalleled. The Volkswagen, known today as the Beetle, which he designed just before the war has been in production for over half a century with well over 21 million sold.

But the unrivalled success of the Volkswagen should not be allowed to overshadow the fact that on the eve of this century, at the age of twenty-five, Porsche was already designing a car with revolutionary, electric, hub-mounted motors, nor that he was responsible for the design of some of the most legendary cars produced by Austro-Daimler, Mercedes-Benz and Steyr before he established his own design office in Stuttgart in December 1930. From here emerged the Volkswagen but also the famous and immensely successful, mid-engined, sixteen-cylinder Auto Union Grand Prix car.

Racing was his passion. In the early years he often raced his cars himself and he firmly believed that racing was essential to the development of road vehicles: his 520 bhp Auto Union Grand Prix car and the original 25 bhp Volkswagen had a surprising number of design features in common.

From the time the Porsche design office was established, Porsche's son Ferry began to work with his father and in the immediate postwar years, while his father was interned by the Allies, he

Porsche

demonstrated his ability by leading the design of a highly advanced, four-wheel drive Grand Prix car for the Italian company Cisitalia. Using mainly Volkswagen components, he also designed and built a two-seater sports car – the Type 356.

Unfortunately Ferdinand Porsche's death in 1951 robbed him of the opportunity to see the company named after him grow under his son's management. Neither did he witness the development of the most famous Porsche car of all – the 911 – which owes a large part of its success to a member of the third Porsche generation. F. A. Porsche, known as Butzi, gave the 911 its inimitable shape which remained largely unchanged for thirty-five years. Nor was Ferdinand Porsche able to enjoy the fantastic boost given to the company's prestige by the series of resounding racing successes of the Porsche 917, designed under the leadership of his grandson Ferdinand Piëch (today President of the Volkswagen Group) and the Types 935, 936 and 956/962 which followed.

Today Porsche is recognised around the world as the most important company specialising in the manufacture of sports cars. But it is also a highly regarded engineering company to which the world's best car, motorcycle and aeroplane manufacturers have recourse for the development of engines and a host of other components.

A fiftieth anniversary is important for any company, but the story of the impact of three generations of the Porsche dynasty on the development of the automobile goes back one hundred years.

Ferdinand Porsche's early career 1898-1923

by Michel Kaltschmid

Ferdinand Porsche was born in 1875 in Maffersdorf, in what is now the Czech Republic. Towards the end of the nineteenth century this isolated Bohemian town, although small, already boasted some industry. Porsche's father was a skilled tinsmith who owned a modest workshop in the town. When the first factories in the area were supplied with electricity in the 1890s, the young Ferdinand Porsche was one of the first employees to take an active interest in the new technology.

He had acquired his technical knowledge from textbooks and had secretly built himself a small laboratory in the attic of the family home. He later attended evening classes at the Imperial trade school in Reichenberg and in 1893 installed electric lighting in the family home. The journeyman-plumber then took his first job as a trainee at Béla Egger United Electric Company. Here he rapidly climbed the ladder and by 1897, at the age of twenty-two, was head of the test section and first assistant in the design department.

The Jacob Lohner Imperial Carriage Works in the Austrian capital Vienna began equipping its coaches and carriages with motors as early as the 1890s. Initial contacts with Daimler, Diesel and Krupp, however, did not prove as successful as the company had hoped. The first Lohner motor car was fitted with a 6 hp pygmy engine made by the French firm Lefèbre-Fessard, but the performance was unsatisfactory. In the same period the first electric motor cars were also being built and Lohner used Egger motors and 80 V/90 Ah batteries weighing 430 kg. The first trial runs, at which Ferdinand Porsche represented the firm Egger, took place in Vienna on 26 June 1898. The test car came to a stop on an uphill gradient – but Ferdinand Porsche solved the problem and the Egger-Lohner was able to tackle roads with a 10 per cent gradient.

Austrian motor cars went on show at the 1898 Jubilee Trade Exhibition in Vienna and included the Marcus car, Lohner's first petrol-engined car and the very same Egger-Lohner electric motor car.

In 1898 Porsche's interest in the electric motor car led him to relinquish his post at Béla Egger and to move to the Lohner works in Vienna. Porsche had recognised the weaknesses of the Egger-Lohner vehicle and set about designing his 2.5 hp wheel hub motor, an internal pole motor which was fitted directly on to the axle on the wheel-hub. In 1899 Lohner car number 24,000 was fitted with two wheel-hub motors as the first Lohner-Porsche car. This motorised carriage was built in record time. Without any intermediate gearing, the power of both 2.5 hp electric motors turning at 120 rpm was transmitted directly to the front wheels. The carriage was therefore drawn rather than propelled, which meant that it did not skid when cornering. A 44-cell storage battery with a capacity of 80 V/300 Ah gave the vehicle a range of 50 km.

1.2

1.1
A four wheel drive version of the Lohner-Porsche car. The vehicle was ordered by a Mr. Hart of Luton. Ferdinand Porsche is in the front passenger seat.

1.2
Ferdinand Porsche chauffeuring the Archduke Franz-Ferdinand in a Lohner-Porsche 'mixte' car on military manoeuvres in 1902.

1.3
Ferdinand Porsche at the wheel of a Lohner-Porsche racing car in 1900.

1.3

1.1

1.4

1.4
Austro-Daimler 'Maja' car, 1906.

The car had kingpin steering, and locking pawls on the rear wheels prevented it from rolling backwards when going uphill. The front wheels were braked electrically, and a mechanical brake was fitted on the rear wheels. The top speed was a heady 50 km/h!

Porsche soon realised that the battery capacity was the decisive factor in the performance of his electric motor cars. For the more powerful 17.5 hp type III motors he used an 88-cell battery which required 220 volts. To charge these, the Lohner company designed a charging trolley with 3.5 hp/2 kW generators. To free the electric motor car from the recurrent need for charging, they built a new type of vehicle called the Semper Vivus. This was a mixed propulsion car in which a 16 hp Austro-Daimler flat-four engine drove a 10 kW/80 V alternator, which supplied the necessary current to the wheel-hub motors.

Lohner exhibited his improved vehicles, including trucks and fire-engines, at the Paris World Fair. By now they could achieve a top speed of 90 km/h and cope with a gradient of 20 per cent. In order to demonstrate the performance of Lohner-Porsche vehicles, the firm took part in numerous races, competitions and hill trials, usually with Ferdinand Porsche himself at the wheel.

The firm was not only successful in producing a growing quantity and wide range of vehicles for the Austrian market; the factory could also point to increasing exports to Germany, France and Denmark. However, Ferdinand Porsche's relationship with Ludwig Lohner was becoming strained; according to Lohner the young designer was spending too much money on design and development. In September 1905 Ferdinand Porsche left the Lohner works in Vienna.

But by now Porsche's name was already well known in engineering circles. His electric motor cars with their racing success, and his mixed propulsion cars, enjoyed an international reputation. Porsche was now required to carry out his military service and as a reserve infantryman in the Austrian army, he was appointed as personal driver to the Archduke Franz-Ferdinand, heir to the Austrian throne. On manoeuvres he proudly drove the Archduke in the Lohner-Porsche he had designed himself, thereby making his military car, in all probability, the world's first 'mobile command post'.

Following his military service, Porsche went to work at the Austro-Daimler company. Links with Austria were already established at the time the Daimler Company was founded in 1890. In 1899 Austro-Daimler was established at Wiener Neustadt, some fifty kilometres to the south of Vienna. Daimler's eldest son Paul took charge of the technical management of the factory and production initially centred on the manufacture of heavy-goods vehicles in which Lohner chassis were used.

In the years 1903-1905 they were already contemplating the manufacture of off-road vehicles with all-wheel drive for the army. When Ferdinand Porsche started work in Wiener Neustadt in 1906 he turned his attention to passenger cars and racing cars. The Maja car became the standard production model. Like Daimler's marque Mercedes, Austro-Daimler's Maja was named after one of the daughters of a successful Austrian businessman, Emile Jellinek. He was a major customer of Daimler in Bad Cannstatt, thereby laying the foundations for the sales success of the cars which he ordered and sold. In Wiener Neustadt the 30 hp standard model was therefore christened the Maja. Ferdinand Porsche designed new motors for this car which he was soon to discard. Finally he decided to produce an 85 hp racing car which was to be powered using the mixed propulsion principle. In 1907 this car, with its wheel-hub motors, reached a top speed of 125 km/h. One exceptional feature of this vehicle was the water-cooled rear breaking system.

Ferdinand Porsche did not let his position as technical manager at Austro-Daimler stop him from taking the wheel himself in reliability trials and races. In 1909 the company took part in the Prinz Heinrich Competition. These reliability trials stretched from Berlin to Budapest via Breslau and on to Munich via Salzburg. The factory entered three cars in the competition, one of them driven by Ferdinand Porsche himself.

That year the team only took the silver medal, which prompted Ferdinand Porsche to design a more powerful engine. Thanks to a streamlined body, the 86 hp 'Big Daimler' with a top speed of 140 km/h took the first three places in the overall class in 1910. Ferdinand Porsche also took part and claimed several victories in the notoriously tough Austrian Alpine competitions, driving vehicles which he had designed – often with his wife as co-driver. Because of the physical risks involved, such a manager-driver combination would be unimaginable today.

Prior to appointing Ferdinand Porsche as chief designer, Austro-Daimler had mainly produced large vehicles. The first small car appeared in 1919 and attracted great interest. This vehicle was equipped with a 16/18 hp four-cylinder engine with universal-shaft drive and one set of brakes for each set of wheels. The side carburettor had water preheating. Again it was Porsche who set about proving the reliability of the small car on a run from Vienna to London.

Even before Porsche took over as technical manager at Austro-Daimler, the company had built electric motor cars and vehicles with mixed petrol-electric propulsion at Wiener Neustadt. These were mainly trucks, buses and fire-engines. It was, however, typical of Ferdinand Porsche to want to explore the limits of this technology. He consequently set about designing a petrol/electrically driven racing car for the Taunus Race in 1907, with a power output of 30/55 hp. In its design this Taunus racing car was years ahead of the competition, but

1.5
A Lohner-Porsche fire-engine from 1904. Austro-Daimler fire-engines employing Porsche's system of hub-mounted motors were the first motorised vehicles used by the London Fire Brigade in 1910.

in trial runs Porsche had an accident and the car could not start the race. The further development of mixed-propulsion technology assumed greater importance for trucks and buses.

Right from the early years of manned flight there was an airfield in Wiener Neustadt where Austrian aviation pioneers such as Igo Etrich undertook test flights. In 1910 Ferdinand Porsche supplied Etrich's biplane with a 40 hp Aero-Daimler engine, derived from the Prinz Heinrich car. A six-cylinder aero-engine, which Porsche designed in 1914, was able to deliver almost 100 hp. The development of these special engines continued up until the end of the First World War in 1918; maximum power outputs of up to 350 hp being achieved with the six-cylinder engines, which even at this early stage had four valves per cylinder. The crowning achievement was probably the twelve-cylinder V-engine with a 30 litre displacement delivering 250, hp built by Ferdinand Porsche. Because the Maria-Theresa Military Academy was located in Wiener Neustadt, Austro-Daimler often received a visit from the Austrian Imperial household when test flights with Daimler engines were undertaken at the Wiener Neustadt airfield.

In 1913 the Daimler works were merged with the Škoda Group. Over the next couple of years, and throughout the First World War, priority was given to the planning and manufacture of vehicles for the army. Ferdinand Porsche found an 80 hp four-cylinder military car with all-wheel drive already completed when he took office at the company in 1906. From this the Type 100 was developed, a six-cylinder engine which delivered 100 hp. With its four-wheel drive and two differential locks, this vehicle was capable of towing 24 tonnes and climbing 25 per cent gradients. It had originally been built as a tractor for hauling 30.5 cm mortar.

As early as 1913 a colonel in the Imperial army, Ottokar von Pagenau, had called, in the *Memoranda on Items of Artillery and Military Engineering*, for a means of transport which would produce high drive, traction and braking performances. The ability to negotiate narrow, twisting mountain roads was a further essential requirement. These conditions could only be fulfilled with the weight distributed between ten axles. In solving this problem, Ferdinand Porsche again opted for a mixed propulsion system: the engine truck containing a six-cylinder engine which drove a generator. The latter in turn fed the wheel-hub motors in the trailer vehicles. The power supply was via a long cable, each trailer being steered by a separate system so that all vehicles ran with the same tracking. Furthermore it was also possible to uncouple the trailers from the traction vehicle and to make them 'follow on' simply via the power supply through the cable, for example on narrow mountain roads or when fording rivers. This brilliant design by Ferdinand Porsche is still in use today: a special tractor-trailer unit of the US Army used in the Arctic is based on the same technical principles. The turning circle of the Landwehr Train was just 12 metres, so that the tractor could even push on the last trailer. In reverse, the train could also be steered from the last trailer. Another stroke of technical genius was the C-train, which also used a mixed propulsion system to transport heavy mortars during the First World War. It had detachable 'road wheels' which could be removed so that the C-train could run on rails. In the view of many experts, Ferdinand Porsche's design was half a century ahead of its time. In 1917, the same year that Ferdinand Porsche was appointed general manager of Austro-Daimler, the Technical University of Vienna awarded him an honorary doctorate.

When the First World War ended in 1918 Ferdinand Porsche returned to building sports cars with even greater enthusiasm. The idea of building a small, manoeuvrable car for racing came from a friend, Alexander 'Sascha', Count Kolowrat. It was originally proposed to fit a

1.1 litre four-cylinder engine in the 775 kg car, which was given the name Sascha. Porsche managed to get the weight of the car down to just 598 kg, which at the time was nothing short of sensational. The engine of the ADS R type had two overhead camshafts.

Four Sascha cars were entered in the Targa Florio in 1922 and were the smallest and lightest cars in the race. With Alfred Neubauer leading the Austro-Daimler racing team, the Sascha cars took first and second places in the small car class and, remarkably, Neubauer's average speed was only 8 km/h slower than that of the overall winner – a Mercedes driven by Masetti, with a far larger and more powerful engine.

A new large car was also developed in the years immediately following the First World War, the AD 617. This was the first heavy and expensive car of the period. The type 617 flat-six engine had a 4.43 litre displacement, was fitted with overhead camshafts driven by vertical driveshafts and delivered 60 hp. For the first time a lightweight construction was used, the crankcase and pistons being made of aluminium alloy with steel cylinder liners inserted. The smooth, harmonious shape of the engine, the so-called 'clean-engine concept', became the trademark of Austro-Daimler engine design. The AD 617 had giant drum brakes on the rear wheels, in addition to a cardan brake operated by a second brake pedal of its own, the chassis and engine of which together weighed approximately 1,000 kg. The car was water-cooled with a finned wheel on the flywheel, which drew the air through the radiator and engine compartment, serving as a cooling air fan. A wide assortment of bodies was built on to the chassis of the AD 617 which later, fitted with front brakes, was called the ADV 617. The ideas and plans of Ferdinand Porsche lived on at Austro-Daimler in Wiener Neustadt for many years after the brilliant designer left the factory.

Shortly after the end of the First World War, and the break up of the Austro-Hungarian Empire, the Austro-Daimler company in Wiener Neustadt left the Škoda Group. The Viennese Bank and Credit Union for Trade and Industry acquired the majority shareholding and the company was headed by Camillo Castiglione. Ferdinand Porsche found it impossible to work with this man. Their differing views on finance and corporate policy made it impossible for Ferdinand Porsche to stay with Austro-Daimler. In the spring of 1924 he took his leave and moved to Stuttgart. Except for a short year as chief designer at Steyr in 1929, Porsche would not return professionally to Austria until after the end of the Second World War, when the world-famous Porsche Type 356, designed by his son Ferry, was born at Gmünd.

Translated by Michael Bettney

1.6
The 'Landwehr' train, 1912.

1.7
Alfred Neubauer at the wheel of an Austro-Daimler Sascha after the Targa Florio in 1922. The third boy from the left is Ferry Porsche.

1.8
Prototype for a road version of the Sascha racing car. Count Alexander Kolowrat, who funded the development of the car, is seen at the wheel.

1.9
Malcolm Campbell racing an Austro-Daimler Sascha at Holme Moss in England in 1923.

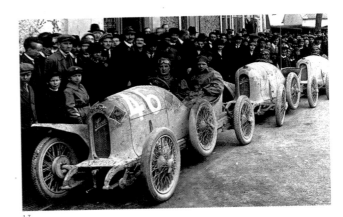

1.7

1.8

Ferdinand Porsche at Daimler-Benz 1923-1928 and 1938-1939

by Karl Ludvigsen

2.1
Christian Werner in the Mercedes
'Kompressor' car which won the
Targa Florio in 1924.

The intense interest in motor racing and small, efficient cars that served Ferdinand Porsche so well in the 1930s did not always benefit his relationships with the Daimler motor company, which fused with Benz in 1926 to become Daimler-Benz. This was the proud company, pioneer of the lightweight high-speed petrol engine that made the motor car possible, that had not hesitated to show the door to Wilhelm Maybach, one of the finest engineers ever to design motor vehicles. The reason? Not because Maybach was insufficiently creative, but because he was too creative. Similar problems would plague some of Porsche's several meetings at the Daimler-Benz headquarters in the Stuttgart suburb of Untertürkheim.

Maybach's successor at Daimler was Paul Daimler, the founder's son. The excellent Mercedes aero-engines of World War One were built under his direction, as were the first supercharged Mercedes cars. But Daimler also led his company down the dead-end street of the Knight sleeve-valve engine. In the last days of 1922 he resigned to take up similar duties at Horch, which planned to strengthen its challenge to Mercedes in the prestige-car market. Ferdinand Porsche, who followed in Daimler's footsteps at Austro-Daimler in 1906, also followed him at Daimler in 1923.

Although he was not officially installed at Untertürkheim until 30 April, Porsche in fact arrived earlier and found himself in the midst of the final preparations for the most ambitious racing effort ever undertaken by Mercedes, a campaign that one of the participants said cost the company an enormous amount of money. It sent a team of three supercharged, two-litre, four-cylinder cars to race 500 miles at Indianapolis in May 1923.

Running as high as third and finishing eighth and eleventh in the Indy 500, the new engines proved their toughness but not their ability to hold a supercharged state of tune. Probing every aspect of their design, frequently driving the test cars himself at the age of forty-eight, the sharp-eyed Ferdinand Porsche dedicated himself to their constant improvement. After his revisions, this two-litre Mercedes scored the fine victory in the Targa Florio on 27 April 1924 for which the cars are celebrated. Cool and relaxed works test-driver Christian Werner mastered his car and the field to win both the Targa Florio and Coppa Florio.

This was a stunning success in one of the most respected races of the day. When Werner, Porsche and the Mercedes returned from Sicily to Stuttgart they were hailed in the square fronting the town hall as conquering heroes. Following a speech of praise from the mayor, Porsche was asked to sign Stuttgart's golden book of high honours. He was also awarded an honorary doctorate by the Stuttgart Technical Institute. It was granted 'in recognition of his outstanding merit in the field of motor car design and particularly as designer of the winning car in the 1924 Targa Florio'.

This was not Porsche's last word on the subject of the ideal racing car to compete under the two-litre Grand Prix racing formula. Four handsome straight-eight Mercedes cars that met that criterion were entered for the Italian Grand Prix on 19 October. The imperturbable Christian Werner would drive one and the very fast Giulio Masetti another. Alfred Neubauer was assigned a third car and the fourth was handled by Count Louis Zborowski.

The main opposition in the 60-lap, 373-mile race was the strong Alfa Romeo P2 team. Sometime Alfa team member Masetti challenged them strongly with his Mercedes, running second on the first lap and then falling to fourth before retiring. Count Zborowski managed a pit stop in spite of clutch problems and returned to the fray, but failed to finish his forty-fourth lap. According to an eyewitness,

2.2

Rudolf Caracciola winning
the 1926 German Grand Prix
at Avus in the Mercedes
Monza car from 1924.

2.3

The chassis of the Mercedes
Monza car, showing the supercharged eight-cylinder engine.

2.3

2.2

coming out of the fast Lesmo turn the Mercedes suddenly snaked and then spun across the road. The car careered against two posts and ended up against a tree, facing in the opposite direction from which it had come. Zborowski was thrown from the car and killed.

This was the tragic end to the only major international race entry made by Porsche's two-litre, eight-cylinder Mercedes. His eight's advanced power unit had tremendous potential that was only partially realised. In the Daimler tradition it used fabricated steel cylinders like its main competitors, Fiat and Alfa Romeo, but it differed from them in retaining the four valves for each cylinder that had worked so well for Daimler in the past. The sodium-cooled valves were inclined in a pent-roof combustion chamber and opened by twin overhead camshafts.

In the development of peak power, Porsche's Roots-super-charged Mercedes eight was outstanding. It produced 170 bhp at 7,000 rpm and was engineered to operate safely to 8,000 rpm, an advance of some 25 per cent over accepted racing engine speeds. Only the French Delage V-12 and a handful of centrifugally super-charged American Miller engines surpassed its output under the two-litre formula that concluded in 1925.

The engine was placed well to the rear in the chassis, more than was customary in other Grand Prix cars. Porsche also defied convention by placing the 25-gallon fuel tank in the space beneath the seats and ahead of the rear axle, where depletion of the fuel would have the least effect on the car's weight distribution. Thus the main weight masses were concentrated toward the centre of this chassis.

It was then, and remained for more than a decade, Ferdinand Porsche's view that such a central grouping of the main masses, which reduced the polar moment of inertia of the car as a whole, made the vehicle less likely to generate the forces in a turn that would act to make one end of the chassis break loose and slide outward. This concept would prove valid in a much later era when tyre designs advanced. But in the context of the chassis design of the 1920s it was more relevant to the handling of this Mercedes that when it did break away in a corner, its low polar moment allowed it to yaw very quickly, so quickly in fact that few drivers could catch it.

One driver able to take advantage of the qualities of Porsche's eight was Rudolf Caracciola, who would become one of the brightest stars in the Mercedes firmament. On 11 July 1926 he drove one, converted with the addition of a vestigial rear seat into a 'sports car', in the German Grand Prix, the first race of that name ever held. It was staged on a four-lane toll highway southwest from Berlin toward Potsdam, known as the Avus. Adding connecting loops at each end of the Avus converted the divided highway into a 12.2-mile track for the Grand Prix.

After 243 miles, and almost three hours of chaotic competition that started in the dry and continued in pelting rain, watched by more than 200,000 Berliners, Caracciola crossed the finishing line exhausted. He and riding mechanic Eugen Salzer were stunned to learn that they had won the first Grand Prix of Germany at the impressive average speed of 83.95 mph. Among the many congratulating Porsche after the victory was an aspiring politician, Adolf Hitler. It was a meeting the apolitical engineer would only vaguely remember.

Just two weeks earlier, Tuesday 29 June 1926 witnessed the creation of Daimler-Benz from the merger of Daimler with one of its major marketplace rivals, Benz & Cie of Mannheim. Henceforth the cars of Daimler-Benz would be known as 'Mercedes-Benz'. And leading the combined range was a powerful six-cylinder model whose design had been one of Ferdinand Porsche's first tasks at Daimler. With the speed that was typical of the era, its first prototypes were ready early in 1924. One was taken to Sicily by Max Sailer during reconnaissance for the Targa Florio. Later in 1924 the motoring world was shown the first large supercharged production Mercedes cars. The new models came in two sizes. The smaller six, of 3,920 cc, was fitted to Type 15/70/100 Mercedes cars that could weigh as much as 5,500 pounds. Although this was a model with much to be modest about, it remained in production through 1929. The larger six, designated the Type 24/100/140, boldly bore the marks of Porsche's authorship on its 6,242 cc engine. Among its traditional Daimler design features were its single overhead camshaft driven by worm gears on a vertical shaft at the rear of the engine and its throttle-pedal-controlled supercharger supplying pressurised air to the carburettor.

From Austro-Daimler Porsche brought a different yet proven technique for cylinder block construction. A one-piece cylinder head was cast in grey iron. The cylinder block was cast in Silumin, one of the lightest aluminium alloys available. Cylinder liners of grey iron were inserted dry into the bores, held in place by flanges at the top.

Placed at the front of the engine, the supercharger was mounted vertically in the classic Daimler manner and circumferentially-finned in the style that Porsche had introduced for the 1924 Targa

2.4
Rudolf Caracciola winning the 1926 German Grand Prix at Avus in the Mercedes Monza car from 1924.

2.5
Otto Merz celebrating a victory at the Nürburging in 1928 with a Mercedes-Benz model S.

2.6
The Mercedes-Benz S series cars were a symbol of wealth and power in the late 1920s.

2.4

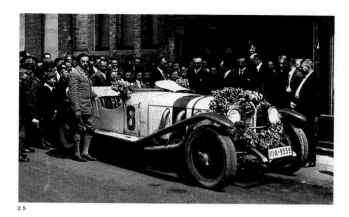

2.5

2.6

Florio two-litre engine. As the car's type designation indicated, the engine was factory-rated at 100 bhp unsupercharged and 140 bhp supercharged, the latter at 3,100 rpm.

Porsche and the Daimler design staff brought the Mercedes star proudly into a new decade of auto engineering on the deeply-veed radiator of the 24/100/140. Born in an era of economic turmoil in Germany, the 24/100/140 became the flagship of the joint marketing efforts of Mercedes and Benz even before those names were inseparably linked by merger.

On a shorter chassis, designated 'K' for *kurz*, Porsche and his fellow racing enthusiasts at Untertürkheim developed an open four-seater tourer body with flowing clamshell fenders and a spare wheel recessed into its sloping tail. Its engine output was increased to 110 bhp unblown at 2,800 rpm and 160 bhp blown at 3,000, a useful improvement, especially when matched with the reduced 4,400-pound weight of the short-chassis car with its sports body.

The high-rigged Model K was raced by the factory and became a favourite of private competitors. But the newborn Daimler-Benz needed something more professional if it were to continue seriously in racing. That it would do this was by no means a foregone conclusion. Though the mid-1920s saw a sharp economic upturn in Germany, the board of directors of the merged auto company hesitated to vote an important share of its earnings to a new racing project.

The influence of Mannheim was particularly negative. Historian K. B. Hopfinger wrote of the former Benz directors now on the Daimler-Benz board: 'Although on account of the financial status of their former company they were "junior" partners, they did not fail to oppose any suggested scheme which was originated by former directors of the Daimler board. It was in fact those former Benz directors who were successful in preventing the company from building any more racing cars until 1934.'[1] This was immensely discouraging to the competition-minded Ferdinand Porsche.

Early in 1927 a stem-to-stern overhaul of the 24/100/140K made it more suitable for racing. The new Model S, for sport, was as close as the engineers could come to a pure racing machine in 1927. It kept the same wheelbase and track as the K but was radically lower. To reduce height and improve weight distribution the engine was moved rearward more than a foot from its Model K location. The normal Model S engine delivered an unblown 120 bhp at 2,800 rpm, rising to 180 bhp at 3,000 with the compressor engaged. With higher compression ratios and benzol fuel, the cars prepared by the factory for racing produced up to 220 bhp.

The big six was further modified for 1928. Its bore was opened out by two millimetres to increase its displacement to 7,069 cc. In this form, with much improved internals, it was fitted during 1928 to Mercedes-Benz cars bearing the immortal SS and SSK designations. Its nominal supercharged rating was 200 bhp at 3,000 rpm. The true SS-model Mercedes-Benz was designed to offer more interior room and to accommodate the best custom bodywork of the era, including the efforts of the company's own coachbuilders at Sindelfingen.

In the hands of the factory and of enthusiastic and wealthy private owners, the SS-engined low-line S racers did well by the three-pointed star that they typically did not carry on the radiator cap in competition. Many of these race-prepared Mercedes-Benz cars had special racing camshafts that increased the supercharged output to 225 bhp at 3,300. Installing a larger compressor boosted the blown figure to 275. The largest supercharger, nicknamed the 'elephant' blower, was normally reserved for factory cars and for yet another extremely fast racing model, the SSK.

2.7
Mercedes-Benz Nürburg, 1928.

2.8
The chassis and engine of the
Mercedes-Benz model SS, 1927.

The popularity of hill-climbing in Germany was such that in mid-1928 a special shorter car was built to be more manageable for this purpose. A chassis frame like that of a Model S was made, but shortened to reduce the wheelbase to 116.1 inches. As a shortened or *kurz* model this was technically an SK, but with a bow to the new bigger engine it was dubbed the SSK. To spectators at the Gabelbach hill on 29 July 1928 it was just a frighteningly fast fenderless Mercedes-Benz driven to a new record by that nice young man from Remagen, Rudolf Caracciola.

Over the winter of 1928-29 a series of SSK cars was laid down, the last of this great line to be designed under Porsche's direction. Intended mainly for racing, for sprint events in the lighter (3,740 pound) SSK chassis the faithful big six yielded even more power. During 1929 and the first years of the 1930s its output was brought to more than 300 bhp at 3,300 rpm with the 'elephant' blower.

Porsche parted company with Daimler-Benz during a stormy board meeting in October 1928. Although their differences were publicly smoothed over, Porsche's exit from the Daimler-Benz design offices was anything but amiable. His lawyer son-in-law Anton Piëch led a law-suit against Daimler-Benz over the dismissal which was settled out of court in 1930. Porsche rented his handsome villa in the Feuerbach hills, with its generous four-car garage and adjoining storeroom, to his successor as technical director, Hans Nibel.

The Swabians had decided not to renew Porsche's contract after experiencing problems with small cars that had come from his team's draughting boards. Ironically, perhaps even maliciously, the problems chiefly arose with models produced at the former Benz plant in Mannheim. One of the most successful of the Mannheim-built cars was the 4.6-litre side-valve Nürburg 460 straight-eight launched at the 1928 Berlin Show. Built long-chassised to accommodate voluminous bodies, this attacked head-on both Paul Daimler's straight-eight Horch and the big American cars that were increasingly popular in the Europe of the 1920s.

Less happy were the fates of the smaller Mannheim-built sixes designed under Porsche's stewardship: the 2,968 cc 12/55 and the 8/38 of 1,988 cc. Both side-valve models were launched in 1926. The smaller six was the more bedevilled, suffering from problems with its valves and gearbox and erratic braking. According to Halwart Schrader, a later audit established that the 8/38 cost Daimler-Benz at least six million Reichsmarks in warranty repairs.

Porsche also expended the company's resources on experiments with even smaller models, about which the Daimler-Benz board was unenthusiastic. One, dubbed the 5/25, was powered by an overhead-valve six of 1,392 cc and was built in 1927 in a test series of thirty cars to be evaluated by company executives. In 1928 Porsche's attention turned to a 1.3-litre four-cylinder prototype of conventional layout as well as a more radical concept: a rear-engined car with independent suspension and a semi-monocoque body powered by an air-cooled flat-opposed four of 1,201 cc. Here was more than a hint of the later Volkswagen.

2.8

2.9

The Daimler-Benz board and Porsche fell out some five years before Adolf Hitler's friend and automotive advisor Jakob Werlin was made a member of that board in December 1933. Werlin had no axe to grind other than the fulfilment of Hitler's desires and the greater glory of Daimler-Benz in the new Third Reich. Thus Werlin kept in touch with Porsche during his visits from Munich, where he ran the Mercedes-Benz branch, to the Daimler-Benz headquarters town of Stuttgart where Porsche had set up his engineering office in 1930.

Thanks in no small measure to the Werlin connection and the pragmatic outlook of the Swabians in charge of Daimler-Benz, a rapprochement between Porsche and Daimler-Benz was engineered in 1937. This was good timing for Porsche, whose racing-car design services Auto Union had decided to dispense with, after its successful 1936 Grand Prix season, in order to make economies. In 1937 Porsche became an engineering consultant to Auto Union's arch-rival Daimler-Benz. The agreement between the two organisations was both broadened and deepened in 1938.

2.10

An important aspect of the new arrangement was the manufacture by Daimler-Benz of thirty prototypes of the new, small, economy car that Porsche was designing for the German Labour Front. This VW30 series was ready for testing at the end of 1937. After many modifications a further batch of forty-four prototypes was built in 1938 as the VW38 series. By July 1939, when the final run of fifty prototypes of the VW39 series was completed by Daimler-Benz, the KdF-Wagen, as it was known, was recognisably the Volkswagen that was destined to become world-famous.

In a technical meeting at Daimler-Benz on 18 March 1937, the views of Ferdinand Porsche on the design of a 1938 Mercedes-Benz Grand Prix racing car were solicited. From 1938 the cars would have to conform to a new formula that fixed the displacement of unsupercharged engines at four litres and supercharged engines at three litres.

Spread out on the conference table at Untertürkheim were drawings of two Porsche proposals designed around a proposed Daimler-Benz three-litre V-12 engine. Both were rear-engined, with swing-axle rear suspension and fuel tanks along the sides. Porsche also prepared a quarter-scale model of an aerodynamic body design for the new G.P. Mercedes-Benz. Tunnel tests credited it with lower drag than a competitive design from Daimler-Benz.

Although Daimler-Benz favoured a front-mounted engine and the power potential of the supercharged three-litre alternative, the unsupercharged engine, potentially far more sparing with fuel and able to skip one or more pit stops, was a menace that they dared not underestimate. Porsche was commissioned to design an unblown four-litre engine that would fit into the same space as the supercharged V-12. On 1 November 1937 Porsche returned to Untertürkheim with the layouts of two startling twenty-four-cylinder power units.

Two different Porsche engine studies were based on the same broad-arrow W-24 bottom end, with three banks of eight cylinders measuring 4,490 cc. One top end was conventional, with two valves

2.9

The chassis and engine
of the Mercedes-Benz land
speed record car, 1939.

2.10

Wind tunnel testing model of
the land speed record car, 1939.

2.11

The chassis of the
Mercedes-Benz land
speed record car, 1939.

per cylinder. The other was decidedly radical, with a bulkier cylinder head design featuring piston-controlled porting, in essence an advanced two-stroke. However, after successful tests of its own supercharged engine, Daimler-Benz decided to cut off the unblown development direction.

Porsche made an important contribution to the supercharged engines as well. The Daimler-Benz engineers knew that their single-stage superchargers were labouring inefficiently at the high boost pressures they were asking them to deliver. They knew that building up the pressure in two stages, first with a large supercharger and then in a smaller one, would be much more efficient.

To explore the potential of a two-stage Roots system for its new V-12, Daimler-Benz commissioned Porsche to design one for evaluation. In its first trials in November 1938 it seemed disappointing. Mounted on an engine that had just completed a run at 430 bhp with its normal single-stage superchargers, the Porsche R108 two-stage kit reduced its peak power to only 380 bhp. Below 5,500 rpm, however, it showed substantially improved power readings, up as much as 12 per cent, thanks to its reduced drive-power demands. Porsche's prototype led to the design of a new Daimler-Benz two-stage system which, used in the 1939 Grand Prix cars, took them to a new round of successes at record average speeds on Europe's classic circuits that were not matched until 1951.

Meanwhile Porsche and Daimler-Benz had been cooperating on another project, one of the most ambitious either ever undertook. It started when Hans Stuck, the driver who had competed successfully in Porsche-designed SSKs and Auto Unions and broken records in the latter, took note of the feverish global acclaim that had been Malcolm Campbell's after his record speed of 301.129 mph in his Bluebird late in 1935. Hans Stuck resolved to bring the land speed record to Germany.

Ferdinand Porsche was instantly excited when Stuck suggested that he design such a car, so much so that he offered to do it free of charge. The big problem, he told Stuck, would be power. Campbell's Bluebird had a single Rolls-Royce engine with 2,500 hp. Porsche told the eager Stuck that he would need at least that much to do the job, preferably 3,000. At that time no German aero-engine even developed 1,000 bhp, or so the world thought. In 1932 Daimler-Benz had begun work on a liquid-cooled V-12 engine for aircraft. Its Daimler-Benz 601 promised a maximum of 1,300 hp; thus Hans Stuck needed two of them. At the Ministry of Aviation, fighter ace Ernst Udet promised him the engines on loan.

Stuck next took his idea and his promises from Porsche and Udet to Wilhelm Kissel at Daimler-Benz. Though now an opponent on the track, Stuck was still well regarded at Untertürkheim. In fact he had been invited to join the Mercedes-Benz team for the 1935 season. Now it was the summer of 1936 and Stuck was asking the Swabians to build for him one of the most expensive automobiles ever conceived.

2.11

Wilhelm Kissel weighed many factors after that first meeting. As K.B. Hopfinger wrote, Kissel 'did not particularly like Porsche, with whom he had some disagreement at the time when Porsche was chief engineer of his company.[2] Nevertheless, Kissel recommended to the Daimler-Benz board that they should undertake the construction of the car to Porsche's design. That way, Neubauer noted, 'we killed two birds with one stone: for we kept the engines under our control and if need be we could still dissociate ourselves a little from this fantastic undertaking.)[3] If it failed, the failure could be blamed on Porsche.

On 22 March 1937, in a meeting at Untertürkheim, Porsche and his associates laid before Max Sailer and Max Wagner the train of thought that now led them to suggest a single-engined car. In every major dimension and design feature it portrayed the car, Type 80 in the project series of the Porsche office, as it was finally built.

Porsche showed the Daimler-Benz men a graph showing the Type 80 reaching its design speed of 550 km/h, 343 mph, in 3.1 miles from rest, assuming that the power available was 2,200 bhp at 3,500 rpm. But the British were not idle. In the autumn of 1938, when parts for the German record car were being machined and delivered to its assembly bay, British L.S.R. rivals staged a staggering show of speed at Utah's Bonneville Salt Flats that forced Porsche back to the drawing board. First George Eyston elevated his own record to 345.2 mph. Then on 15 September John Cobb lifted it to 350.1 mph with his new twin-Napier-engined Railton Mobil Special. Eyston topped this the following day with 357.3 mph. At 575.1 km/h this was rather faster than the Type 80's original design target of 550 km/h.

Porsche, ever adaptable, produced a new scenario for the Type 80. He now aimed for a speed of 373 mph, 600 km/h, to be reached after 3.7 miles of acceleration, an extremely rapid rate by L.S.R. standards, followed by a braking distance of 1.4 miles. For this, Porsche said, he would need 3,000 hp. Could Daimler-Benz oblige? It could and would, came the reply, with an engine in its early development stages, the Daimler-Benz 603. This new V-12 was 31 per cent larger than the Daimler-Benz 601 at 44,500 cc.

Porsche and his chief engineer Karl Rabe remained faithful to their patented trailing links and transverse torsion bars for the front end of the Type 80. In search of maximum traction with low tyre loadings, the Porsche men decided to use four drive wheels at the rear of the Type 80. They were sprung by swing axles whose detail design was carried over with little change from that of the Porsche-designed sixteen-cylinder Auto Union racing cars.

There were no gears to shift in the Type 80. Porsche had concluded that the ample torque of the huge Daimler-Benz 603 was sufficient to bring the car up to speed with the help of a multiple-disc 'heat-storing' clutch. With the clutch fully engaged at some 100 mph, Hans Stuck would have been able to press the throttle to the floor without worrying about spinning the rear wheels. Some fifty years in advance of its time, Porsche thus designed an automatic slip-controller that was a mechanical counterpart of the ASR systems that helped Grand Prix drivers in the early 1990s.

On 12 October 1939 the Type 80 chassis was placed on the wheel-driven dynamometer of the racing department for a trial under power. Work still remained to be done on the body, including its finish-riveting and its final fitting at all mounting points to the chassis. The Type 80 was about a month away from readiness for a trial on the road. A note had already gone to Hans Stuck advising him to stand by for the first test drive.

By the end of 1939 it was clear that this would not happen. When Stuck visited the factory he was told what so many in Germany

2.12
The Mercedes-Benz land speed record car, 1939.

thought was true at that time: 'The war will be over in three months, and then you can begin again at once!' Not months but years became the measure of that war.

Under his contract with Daimler-Benz, Porsche carried out other engineering projects in the 1938-39 period, including a limited-slip differential, a coach suspension, and hydraulic transmission. Assigned the wartime role of tank czar by Albert Speer, Ferdinand Porsche continued to have contacts with Daimler-Benz but not directly on engineering projects.

The few years left to Porsche in the postwar chaos were not enough for him to re-establish a relationship with the company he most respected. K.B. Hopfinger wrote that Porsche 'always held Daimler-Benz in very high esteem and regarded the time when he was their technical director and chief engineer as one of the most interesting in his career.' That esteem continues to be shared between the Porsche and Daimler-Benz companies, neighbouring innovators and now car producers in the city of Stuttgart.

Acknowledgement:
Some of the above text is adapted from that in the author's history of the Mercedes-Benz sports and racing cars, *Mercedes-Benz Quicksilver Century*, published by Transport Bookman, Isleworth, 1995.

Notes
1 K.B. Hopfinger, *Beyond Expectation, The Volkswagen Story*, London, 1962, p.39
2 ibid., p.102
3 unpublished document, Mercedes-Benz archive

2.12

Ferdinand Porsche
and the Auto Union Grand
Prix cars, 1932-1938

by Doug Nye

In order to understand Ferdinand Porsche's role in the story of the original series Auto Union Grand Prix cars, one must first appreciate the background to the project itself. On 12 October 1932, the governing body of world motor sport – the Association Internationale des Automobile Clubs Reconnus or AIACR – published its changes to the Grand Prix regulations.

From its earliest days Grand Prix racing imposed a heavy financial burden upon participating motor companies. The expenditure would be justified in terms of sales promotion, technical advance, and both corporate and national prestige. The Great Depression of 1930-32 changed all that. As sales collapsed and incomes plummeted, Grand Prix racing became largely an arena in which wealthy private owners fiddled while Rome burned. In order to encourage full starting grids, race promoters had opened their Grand Prix events to almost any kind of car.

Into the 1930s ever-larger engines and ever-increasing power were perceived as the passport to racing success. Bugatti built a 4.9-litre straight-eight Grand Prix car. Maserati produced a four-litre V16 by combining two supercharged engines upon a common crankcase. Alfa Romeo mounted two of their six-cylinder engines side by side in their Tipo A single-seater. Such designs could be very fast, but also very heavy, cumbersome and dangerous.

The AIACR wanted to promote a safe, affordable and popular Grand Prix class for slower, simpler cars which were cheaper to produce and to operate. This, it was hoped, would encourage more competitors and therefore more entertainment for the paying public.

The new rules for the three Grand Prix racing seasons of 1934-36 would pass into posterity as 'the 750 kg Formula', named after its primary restriction. No Grand Prix car would be permitted a bare weight exceeding 750 kg. To verify this 'bare weight' competing cars were to be weighed without fuel, oil, tyres or driver. The AIACR believed this recipe would automatically restrict engine size to approximately three litres, and thereby engine output to only 250 hp. But they had not reckoned with the ground-breaking technology being developed by Daimler-Benz and Auto Union, and in particular that of designers of the calibre of Ferdinand Porsche.

The Auto Union marque was born in 1932 of the fusion of four rival car companies: DKW, Audi, Horch and Wanderer. Each of these had been acquired in turn by the industrialist Jörgen Skafte Rasmussen.

In the previous year Ferdinand Porsche had established his own design consultancy and had received his first commission from one of the future Auto Union companies, Wanderer, to design a medium-range production saloon. His staff consisted of eight Austrians: his right-hand man Karl Rabe, Karl Fröhlich, Josef Kales, Erwin Komenda, Josef Mickl, Franz Reimspieß, Josef Zahradnik and Porsche's faithful chauffeur and helper Joseph Goldinger, who had worked with him since Austro-Daimler days in 1910. Porsche's son, Ferry, who had grown up with cars and was to prove as talented a designer as his father, was also on the staff from the outset. The company's business manager was Adolf Rosenberger, a former amateur racing driver who had campaigned for financial backing to race the Mercedes-Benz SS-series cars that Porsche had designed in the late 1920s.

Ferdinand Porsche had always been a motor-racing enthusiast, seeing it as an invaluable proving ground for advanced technology. By October 1932 his consultancy was doing well, and as he considered news of the AIACR's 750 kg Formula his imagination ran riot at the prospect of unrestricted capacity.

Porsche had always been in favour of independent suspension. His fertile mind quickly grasped the unintended possibilities of the new maximum-weight Formula, for within that 750 Kg limit his team could surely create a large-capacity, high-powered racing car of radical design, with such innovations as all-independent suspension and hydraulic brakes to combat French and Italian state-of-the-art beam axles, rod and cable brakes and heavyweight engine technologies. Such a German Grand Prix contender could dominate the field. On 1 November 1932 Porsche added a High Performance Vehicle Development department to his consultancy to investigate, design, develop and race a 750 kg Formula Grand Prix car.

In the first two weeks of November, Porsche, Kales and Rabe laid out a startling Grand Prix car design with a sixteen-cylinder power unit mounted behind the driver in a simple chassis comprising twin, large-diameter parallel tubes. Kales' supercharged engine featured 68 mm bore, 75 mm stroke, for 4,358 cc and was to run at a comfortable 4,500 rpm. Rabe designed the suspension and running gear, and by July 1933 the consultancy's drawings for this 'P-Wagen' were complete.

Meanwhile, Porsche and Rosenberger tried to gain the necessary support to translate their ideas into hardware. Initial negotiations yielded little, until former European Mountain Champion driver, the Austrian Hans Stuck, became an investor and, more significantly, took the opportunity of a meeting with Hitler to extol the potential of Porsche's new idea.

3.2

Grand Prix racing ambitions had been voiced to Hitler not only by Hans Stuck on behalf of Porsche, but also by Daimler-Benz's Munich branch manager, Jakob Werlin. Hitler was already an enthusiast. Werlin extolled state support for new Grand Prix cars in order to project national prestige beyond German borders. As a result of these discussions the Transport Minister Brandenburg announced a state bounty for the manufacturer of a German Grand Prix racing car.

He offered 450,000 Reichsmarks per year, plus significant bonuses for first, second and third-place finishes. The designers and engineers at Daimler-Benz and at Auto Union knew that the programme would cost far more. Regardless, both declared their intention to go into Grand Prix battle. Auto Union signed a design and development deal with Porsche. Prudently, their agreement was conditional. Porsche's design would only be accepted if it could lap Berlin's Avus track at an average speed of 200 km/h.

At the Horch factory in Zwickau the car, which was given the name Auto Union A-Type, was built under Porsche's direction. The prototype was first test-driven there in October 1933, just eleven months after its inception, and was tested more intensively on the Nürburgring South Circuit on 13 November by Hans Stuck and Prince Hermann zu Leiningen. Stuck was happy to tackle the qualification test at Avus and on 12 January 1934 he hammered the strange, fish-like car, with its rear fuselage skinned in drum-tight fabric, round the speedway for an hour. No problems were encountered and the car was timed at 275 km/h along the straights and averaged 224.8 km/h for the hour.

The Auto Union Directors were ecstatic. Their new Grand Prix car received blanket media coverage and within days the Berlin Motor Show opened with the German cars from Auto Union and Daimler-Benz its sensational centrepiece. Even before its first race Auto Union had become a name familiar not only to every German, but to expectant racing enthusiasts worldwide.

Ferdinand Porsche would preside at all Auto Union events, as consultant chief engineer, to whom the race engineers would refer rather than be formally answerable. The team's racing debut followed at Avus on 27 May 1934. With Hitler watching, three A-Type Auto Unions faced Italy's Alfa Romeos. Stuck led by 1 minute 25 seconds before being forced to retire due to clutch-slip. August Momberger's

3.3

3.4

3.1

H.P. Muller in the Auto Union
C-Type car at the Donington
Grand Prix in 1937.

3.2

Hitler congratulating Rudolf
Caracciola at the 1936 Berlin
Motor Show.

3.3

H.P. Muller in the C-Type car,
1937.

3.4

An Auto Union C-Type car
in Long Island for the 1937
Vanderbilt Cup. Ferdinand
Porsche is directly behind
the driver.

was the only Auto Union to complete the race, in third place. In the Eifel races, at the Nürburgring, Daimler-Benz beat Stuck and the Auto Union car into second place. The major French Grand Prix followed at Montlhéry, where Stuck led for thirty-two impressive laps before retirement. Alfa Romeo's outdated cars could still outlast the new German vehicles, but could not outrun them.

By the time the German Grand Prix took place at the Nürburgring, Ferdinand Porsche's ongoing development work with the Chemnitz racing team built in reliability to match the engine's pace, and Hans Stuck won outright by more than two minutes, a sensational success for all concerned.

Daimler-Benz won its first major event at Pescara in Italy. At Berne, in the Swiss Grand Prix, Stuck's masterly wet-weather driving proved unbeatable. His team-mate Momberger came second. Stuck and Leiningen then shared the second-placed car in the Italian Grand Prix, and fourth in Spain. Stuck completed Auto Union's excellent debut season with victory in the Czechoslovak Grand Prix at Brno. The Austrian driver also won the Kesselberg, Freiburg and Mont Ventoux mountain climbs in the new Auto Union cars. To emphasise their prodigious potential Stuck broke a number of records at Avus, raising the standing-start 50 km record to 250.35 km/h and the standing-start kilometre to 168.95 km/h.

The original A-Type design was modified to create the 1935 B-Type version. Tail-pipe exhaust systems replaced the original abbreviated stubs, fabric side-panelling was replaced with light-alloy sheet, cooling systems were modified with external pipes instead of the original routing through the chassis tubes (often nearly cooking the driver). The rear suspension's heavy transverse leaf spring was also replaced by longitudinal torsion bars. During the next season the engine's bigend bearings would be changed from plain-type to rollers, a Hirth system built-up crankshaft replacing the original one-piece to enable each roller bearing to be slipped into place.

The bore and stroke were both enlarged from the original 68 mm x 75 mm to 72.5 mm x 75 mm, increasing displacement from 4358 cc to 4950 cc. Supercharged at 11 lbs per square inch, the engine output reached 375 bhp at 4,800 rpm and the torque rose from 391 lb/ft at 2,700 rpm to a lung-punching 478 lb/ft at 3,000 rpm. These engine improvements raised the car's maximum speed from approximately 283 to 300 km/h.

For the 1935 season, Auto Union's racing director Dr Karl Feuereissen signed up the famed Italian driver Achille Varzi. He enjoyed a triumphant Auto Union debut at Tunis, but at Tripolione one of his tyres burst and he finished second behind Daimler-Benz, whose team

3.6

3.5
An Auto Union car with streamlined bodywork participating in a
speed test on the autobahn near
Frankfurt, c.1937.

3.6
Bernd Rosemeyer in the
Auto Union C-Type car, 1936.

now assumed the upper hand. At the Avus races, Hans Stuck won his heat but lost the final because of more tyre trouble, Varzi finished third and Leiningen and a new recruit, Bernd Rosemeyer, both retired.

Bernd Rosemeyer's skills had been superbly honed by motor-cycle racing. He had never driven another Grand Prix car and as far as he was concerned they probably all handled like Porsche's Auto Union car. He adapted naturally to responses in the car which drivers experi-enced in traditional front-engined racing cars often found bewilderingly alien. In particular, Porsche's favoured swing-axle rear suspension made these tail-heavy, monstrously powerful cars very difficult to drive near their ultimate cornering limits. The narrow and extremely hard Continental racing tyres were designed purely to stave off wear and an ultimate burst as long as possible. Under high lateral loads the swing-axle suspension tended to minimise further the tyres' already narrow contact area. With almost 500 ft/lbs torque this would unleash runaway wheelspin; the long tail would wag furiously, and the driver would have to fight to retain control.

With Porsche's approval, two Hirth crank engines, retaining the 72.5 mm bore but introducing a stroke enlarged from 75 to 85 mm, were installed for the French Grand Prix, displacing 5,600 cc, but the cars were forced to retire due to lubrication, spark-plug and brake problems. Only one Auto Union finished, in fifth place, so Porsche's team conserved its energies in preparing for the important German Grand Prix. In this race Hans Stuck was beaten into second place, not by the Daimler-Benz team, which might have been expected, but by the Italian Tazio Nuvolari's obsolescent Alfa Romeo. However, at Pescara, Varzi and Rosemeyer finished first and second for Auto Union and, along the coastal Montesilvano straight, Varzi's car achieved 305 km/h. The Auto Union board was naturally disappointed at the sparse successes of 1935, but agreed to authorise a continuing programme for 1936, which should have been the 750 kg Formula's final year.

Porsche and his team developed a new car, the C-Type, with 75 mm bore and 85 mm stroke displacing a full 6,010 cc and delivering 520 bhp at 5,000 rpm, 85 bhp per litre and torque now peaking at 630 lb/ft at a mere 2,500 rpm. At that crankshaft speed the V16 engine still developed 300 hp. An even wilder R-Type unit was produced, with 87 mm bore for 6,330 cc and 545 bhp, which was mainly used for record-breaking attempts.

Daimler-Benz's Grand Prix car development stumbled that sea-son, opening a door for Auto Union. Although the state grants and bonus system had been updated, it never even came close to covering the costs of racing. However, it is unlikely that Auto Union or Daimler-Benz would have bothered without its impetus or without the resulting close relationships with government ministries. Auto Union could never hope to match the finances of Daimler-Benz, whose racing policy was to do the job first and find the funds later. This financial inequality inevitably influenced the design process of the two competing companies.

Almost every single component of the Daimler-Benz Grand Prix cars was machined, ground, drilled or in some way fine-finished, often by hand, even in its least accessible corners. The designers would constantly set the machinists and fabricators seemingly impossible challenges, which in almost every case were met. The cost in man-hours, machine capability and availability as much as in premium-class material was plainly no obstacle. By contrast, Porsche pursued a prag-matic and selective design and development policy. Where matching Daimler-Benz in design, manufacture and finish was genuinely neces-sary, or would pay dividends, the investment would be made. Where function was of paramount importance and finish irrelevant, corners were cut.

Despite its greater financial resources, nothing could save Daimler-Benz from crushing defeat throughout 1936 by the combination of Auto Union's C-Type car and Bernd Rosemeyer's mercurial driving talents. Varzi's second Auto Union season began badly when his car somersaulted at approximately 290 km/h during the Tunis Grand Prix, but he survived. Ernst von Delius joined the team in Barcelona and finished fourth. At the Eifel races, in swirling mist and drizzle, with visibility often down to 50 metres or less, Rosemeyer took a two-minute lead, and won brilliantly.

3.7

In Hungary Nuvolari narrowly beat Rosemeyer, but the Auto Union driver won the all-important German Grand Prix. In both the Coppa Acerbo race at Pescara and the Swiss Grand Prix the Auto Union cars came first, second and third. Rosemeyer also won the Italian Grand Prix. He became European Champion – the 1930s equivalent of the modern Drivers' World Champion title – and for good measure won the Freiburg mountain climb, breaking Hans Stuck's record.

Meanwhile, the AIACR had declared a replacement Grand Prix Formula to take effect in 1937, but they had given such little notice that all the competing manufacturers sought, and received, a one-year extension of the existing Formula, postponing the new rules until 1938.

Auto Union decided against developing its C-Type cars any further. Following the successes of 1936 it was clear that they would be good enough for the coming season. All available funding was invested instead in a new replacement design for the 1938-40 Formula, which demanded engines of only three litres if supercharged or 4.5 litres if unsupercharged, in cars weighing essentially a minimum of 850 kg, 100 kg more than the old maximum limit.

Personal and political problems were to alter the make-up of the Auto Union racing team. Hans Stuck was long past his prime and became the victim of Nazi propaganda – he was being pilloried because he had a Jewish wife. Varzi was becoming increasingly addicted to morphine. Auto Union's future successes would, generally speaking, be secured by a new generation of drivers and, of course, the young Bernd Rosemeyer.

At the start of the year two cars were shipped to South Africa for Rosemeyer and von Delius, who won the minor handicap Grosvenor Grand Prix at Cape Town. Rosemeyer subsequently won the Eifel races, the Vanderbilt Cup on Long Island, the Coppa Acerbo and the Donington Grand Prix, all against the strongest-ever Daimler-Benz opposition from the formidable Type W125 cars.

Another new team driver, Rudolf Hasse, won the 1937 Belgian Grand Prix and Stuck won the La Turbie and Freiburg mountain climbs. However, 1937 witnessed a disaster for the Auto Union team when Ernst von Delius lost his life in a high-speed collision with a Daimler-Benz car in the German Grand Prix. Bernd Rosemeyer's victory in the Donington Grand Prix saw Auto Union win the last 750 kg Formula race to be held, a grand finale to an extraordinary era in which Auto Union had frequently shone, presaging a rear-engined motor racing future which would not materialise for more than twenty years.

The amount of time that Porsche was able to devote to Auto Union and the racing team during 1937 decreased substantially. He had visited America briefly in 1936, travelling only with his nephew Ghislaine Kaes, who acted as his personal secretary. Porsche was given the red carpet treatment by American motor manufacturers. He bought Packard's latest eight-cylinder car and drove it through America before returning to Germany via England, where he visited the Austin factory.

He returned to America in 1937, accompanied by Jakob Werlin; Otto Dieckhoff, director of Auto Union; Dr Bodo Lafferentz, the official responsible to the German Labour Front for the Volkswagen project,

3.7
Bernd Rosemeyer after winning
the 1937 Donington Grand Prix.
With him is the Auto Union chief
engineer, Robert Eberan von
Eberhorst.

3.8
The sixteen-cylinder engines
of the C-Type cars.

and his son Ferry. They visited Henry Ford to investigate if any of his experience in manufacturing the Model T would be applicable to building the Volkswagen.

As Porsche's commitment to the development of the Volkswagen grew, he handed over responsibility for the Auto Union Grand Prix cars to Dr Robert Eberan von Eberhorst, a young Viennese engineer who was a former lecturer at the Dresden Technical Institute, and a friend and admirer of Porsche. He and Werner Strobel now headed an in-house design team and completed the three litre V12 D-Type cars for the 1938 and 1939 seasons.

On 28 January 1938 Bernd Rosemeyer was killed when his Auto Union car crashed during a record attempt on the Frankfurt-Darmstadt autobahn. It was the first time Dr Porsche had not been present at a record attempt in one of 'his' Auto Unions. It was evidence of the end of the relationship, a tragedy which hit the old man, now sixty-three, very hard. But his energies were by this time fully engaged with the Volkswagen project and with a commission from his old employer and recent rival Daimler-Benz to design a land speed record car.

3.8

The Volkswagen 1933-1945 – the development of the people's car.

By Bernd Wiersch

Although the motor car was invented by Gottlieb Daimler and Karl Benz in 1886 as the new means of transport for the next century, it was by no means universally accepted as such by the public at large. Initially a few firms experimented with this new vehicle, but they often lacked the technical expertise or the capital to produce cars in larger numbers. The first cars resembled carriages and could, generally speaking, only be afforded by those who in earlier years had owned horse-drawn carriages. No concerted marketing campaign was mounted to attract new customers – at least not in Germany – because as a rule the price was much too high. In those days virtually no one in Germany thought of the car as a mass mode of transport – it was arguably just a plaything for a small number of well-off people.

Although attempts were made in Germany around the turn of the century to develop small cars, most designers set about it entirely the wrong way. They took a big car as their model and, in order to save costs, omitted those parts thought not to be absolutely essential in a car, such as the reverse gear, the suspension, or other features which we today regard as indispensable to the operating reliability of a vehicle.

Nor did the available space match the needs of potential customers. In those days the average family in Germany had more than four members, whereas these small cars were usually designed with only enough space for two people. The vehicles were therefore quite unsuitable for a family. Some manufacturers resorted to providing open seats at the rear of the car. Normally there was no space for luggage, so special trunks were strapped to the rear of the car with the aid of a luggage rack. However, this gave the car a somewhat peculiar appearance.

In the first two decades of this century car design, as we know it today, did not exist. Until the turn of the century cars were modelled on the horse-drawn carriage. The engine was usually located under the rear bench seat and transmitted its power to the rear wheels by means of drive belts or chains. People in the nascent automobile industry then realised that the engine belonged at the front, for after all on a horse-drawn carriage the horses were also at the front. The drive, however, was still transmitted to the rear wheels. This development was a great step forward in the design and use of cars. Passengers now sat in the back and no longer came into direct contact with the technology – people still kept a chauffeur to drive and service the car – and car bodies were now enclosed boxes with windows which afforded their occupants ample space and comfort. However, that was only the case for big, expensive cars. Although designers of small cars tried to match this and to keep pace with developments, the selling price always imposed restrictions. Savings had to be made and it was not only the engineering but also the comfort of the passenger that was sacrificed.

The many attempts that were made in Germany to extend motoring to a wider public generally foundered on these criteria and each model was only produced in modest quantities. The small car manufactured in the largest quantities was the Hanomag Kommissbrot, of which at least 15,775 were sold, making it the most common car on German roads during the 1920s. In the first five years of that decade there were 116 new entrants to the motor vehicle industry but also 104 insolvencies in this sector. In the second half of the decade, however, there was a disastrous shift in the balance with approximately seventeen new firms but seventy-three insolvencies. The number of firms shrank from eighty-five in the first half of the 1920s to twenty-nine in the second half. These companies turned out an annual total of between 40,000 and 100,000 cars, which is indicative of the average capacity and hence the viability of the factories.

4.3

4.3
Testing the Volkswagen
prototypes in 1937. On the
right is Hans Klauser, who
became manager of the
Porsche factory in Stuttgart
in 1950.

4.4
Ferdinand Porsche showing
Hitler the scale model of
the Volkswagen which was
presented to him on his
birthday in 1939.

In the 1920s Ferdinand Porsche turned his attention to the small car, but one with reasonable standards of performance, engineering and comfort. He made his first attempt at Austro-Daimler with the Sascha sports car, which he regarded as a trial venture for a standard road version. For Porsche the most important aspect of this design was a balanced power-to-weight ratio, so that the car would be able to cope with all potential traffic situations. Regrettably this initial design wasn't pursued because Austro-Daimler was committed to the market for luxury cars. For the time being the concept of the small car seemed to have folded altogether in Germany.

Before the small car for the masses could become a reality something had to happen on the German political stage. The new Nazi government which came to power in 1933 made the motor car and the motor vehicle industry one of the key elements in its programme. It realised that both economic and political capital could be made from the extension of motoring to a wider public, and promoted these ideas in a variety of ways. The German Chancellor, Adolf Hitler, himself a motoring fan although he did not hold a licence, personally took up the idea of universal motor transport and immediately after coming to power spoke at the Berlin Motor Show about the problem of making cars available to the general public, drawing particular attention to German deficiencies in this sector.

Thus Ferdinand Porsche was able to submit his ideas for a small car to the German government before the end of 1933, finding Hitler very receptive. On 17 January 1934 he put his proposals for a 'people's car' into concrete terms in a Memo concerning the German Volkswagen which outlined five major requirements for the vehicle:

1. The best possible suspension and road holding.
2. A top speed of approximately 100 km/h.
3. An ability to climb gradients of approximately 30 per cent.
4. A totally enclosed body for the purposes of private transport.
5. The lowest possible purchase price and lowest possible running costs.

In his memo Porsche also specified the technical data:

Track	1,200 mm
Wheelbase	2,500 mm
Maximum output	26 hp
Maximum engine speed	3,500 rpm
Unladen weight	650 kg
Price	1,550 Reichsmarks
Maximum speed	100 km/h
Hill climbing ability	30 per cent
Fuel consumption	8 litres/100 km
Vehicle type	fully floating axle

The technical parameters were thereby defined and after a brief interval – doubtless not entirely without some political pressure – a contract was signed in the summer of 1934 between Porsche's design consultancy and the National Association of the Motor Vehicle Industry for the design of a Volkswagen prototype. The terms and conditions laid down, however, were anything but attractive to Ferdinand Porsche, because the motor manufacturers in the National Association were naturally not very pleased that an independent engineering design consultancy had been appointed to develop what was effectively a competing product using their money.

The most important clauses in the contract were those which dealt with the money available and the time allowed in which to complete the prototype. The contract stipulated a total of 200,000 Reichsmarks in development costs over a design phase lasting ten months, clear evidence of a critical, indeed almost dismissive, attitude on the part of the National Association.

Ferdinand Porsche now seemed to have achieved his heartfelt aims, but the work and the problems were only just beginning. The impossibly low sales price for the Volkswagen of 990 Reichsmarks, dictated by political pressures, proved to be a particularly irksome constraint on the designer, who was a perfectionist.

It became both a yardstick and a stumbling block on which many a good technical idea foundered during the design phase. Any half-realistic estimate, on which Ferdinand Porsche naturally had to base his development, would have shown that the unit production costs alone would have amounted to this sum, leaving no profit for the manufacturer and no budget for marketing and sales.

The short time-span of just ten months which the contract allowed for completion of the first prototype was also completely unrealistic and had to be constantly extended. Problems arose at every turn, in the detailed design of the car, in obtaining materials and with

4.4

the materials themselves. Numerous technical alternatives were devised, costed and rejected again. As a result, it would take another four years before the Volkswagen was ready for series production in the form envisaged by Ferdinand Porsche and his staff.

Despite these adverse conditions, Ferdinand Porsche set about putting his ideas into practice. The first prototype of the Volkswagen, which was assembled more or less by hand in the private garage annexed to Porsche's villa in Stuttgart, ran under its own power towards the end of 1935, when it clearly began to take shape both technically and visually. For reasons of cost the principle of the rear-mounted engine with drive to the rear wheels was pursued. Porsche had first experimented with a similar design in 1932 when three proto-types of a Kleinwagen (literally small car) were made by the motorcycle manufacturer Zündapp, based on designs submitted to them by Porsche. These were tested but did not reach production stage. A second prototype designed by Porsche and built for another motorcycle company, NSU, in 1934 also failed to reach production. However, during tests the four-cylinder, horizontally-opposed (flat-four) engine had acquitted itself sufficiently well ultimately to be fitted in the series production Volkswagen, scaled down from a displacement of 1.6 litres to just under one.

The prototype Volkswagen had a very advanced aerodynamic design, for which Erwin Komenda was responsible. In the USA the science of aerodynamics was gaining ground in motor vehicle design following successes in the aircraft industry. In Germany the first experiments in the aerodynamic styling of vehicle bodies had been performed

4.6

4.7

4.5

by Baron Koenig-Fachsenfeld, Edmund Rumpler and others without the benefit of a wind tunnel. The process was initially a purely instinctive one because there were no empirical values available. The aim of using aerodynamics in motor car design was to minimise wind resistance and therefore increase speed and reduce fuel consumption.

These ideas were well suited to Porsche's concept because the Volkswagen had to appeal to potential customers whose annual earnings were very low. The shape of the Volkswagen was first tested on scale models in the wind tunnel at the University of Stuttgart and was finalised in a larger wind tunnel at Berlin-Adlershof. The Volkswagen was the first car to be manufactured in Germany with the benefit of an aerodynamically shaped body.

The advanced features of Porsche's design also extended to the engineering. The engine had to be able to power the car at relatively high speeds on the newly designed autobahns, but should not fall behind on hilly or mountainous routes, which called for a power output of approximately 25 hp. For Porsche there were many ways of achieving this. The most favoured solution was the two-stroke engine – not least because of the favourable experience which the German manufacturer DKW had had with this design. Twin-cylinder, two-stroke engines were undergoing just as much development as four-cylinder engines, but all trials with the various types which Porsche was developing posed problems at full throttle and were sooner or later discarded from the design programme.

The only other design solution was relatively expensive but one which Porsche favoured: the four-cylinder, horizontally-opposed engine with air cooling and an output of 24 hp, which had been used in the NSU prototype, met the requirements and was developed into the series production engine. The drawback was that it was not cheap to manufacture, but for Ferdinand Porsche this was no real argument for not developing this engine further. Ultimately there was also pressure from his clients who, after approximately eighteen months design time, finally wanted to see a finished prototype.

With the chassis, too, Porsche was not prepared to make any kind of compromise which might adversely affect the car's handling. From the outset he decided in favour of a platform frame with a centre tunnel to take the control cables which forked in the rear section of the car, in order to accommodate the engine. The independent suspension which, thanks to the torsion bar suspension that was patented in 1931 by Porsche, was also a fixed element of his design concept from the outset.

Once the first prototypes had been completed at the end of 1935, Porsche and his colleagues set about thoroughly testing them for reliability. The Volkswagen would have to prove itself in day-to-day service, and in order to test this it was necessary to subject the vehicles to extreme stresses. Here Porsche would allow no compromise.

In order to test the full-load endurance of the engines they drove them on the autobahn from Stuttgart to Bad Nauheim and back again – a distance of 200 kilometres in either direction – wherever possible at top speed. Any problems that occurred were generally attended to there and then by the test drivers, that is Porsche's colleagues. If, in exceptional cases, this was not possible, the prototypes were towed back to Stuttgart and repaired overnight by the drivers, who then had to drive again next morning. Working days of sixteen hours or more were the rule rather than the exception.

For tests under normal road conditions the twisting and occasionally very steep roads in the Black Forest near Stuttgart proved particularly suitable. The Kniebis and the Zuflucht were two markedly stiff climbs that had to be negotiated. On these stretches drivers had to use all the engine speed ranges and all the gears. If these road conditions were not sufficiently testing, the drivers took the cars into the Austrian Alps. The Großglockner and the Katschberg mountain passes were the preferred test routes, on which gradients of up to 24 per cent demanded everything of the cars. At the time there were no steeper roads in Europe passable by cars.

The trial phase was constantly monitored by engineers from the National Association of the Motor Vehicle Industry, who represented rival motor manufacturers and as such were extremely critical. The established manufacturers showed little affection for the vehicle, since they saw it as a serious competitor to their own small cars.

From October to December 1936 the first three prototypes were each subjected to a continuous test over a distance of 50,000 kilometres under mixed driving conditions. The overall verdict on this test was very supportive of the designer and his staff and was summarised as follows:

'The design has so far proved effective. The test cars have generally proven themselves on the 50,000 km run. Although a number of faults occurred and defects came to light, these were all of a minor nature and can almost certainly be rectified without great difficulty. Various assemblies such as front axles and brakes still require thorough testing. Fuel and oil consumption is within satisfactory limits. The car offers good performance and handling. The vehicle has accordingly shown characteristics which indicate that further development is to be recommended. It is anticipated that the next thirty test cars, currently being manufactured in a proper motor vehicle factory [Daimler-Benz] equipped with all modern facilities and drawing on the experience gained in test runs, will produce significantly better results in a new endurance trial carried out on the same systematic lines.'[1]

This assumption was borne out by the next prototypes which were driven over a total of 2.4 million kilometres before they were destroyed in 1942. It can safely be maintained that the Volkswagen was the most thoroughly tested car of its day.

The first civilian Volkswagens were due to come off the production lines at the newly built and virtually completed factory at Wolfsburg near the small town of Fallersleben in the autumn of 1939. Prospective customers had been encouraged to join a savings scheme, and more than 300,000 people had paid in full for their car. However, the outbreak of the Second World War on 1 September 1939 dashed the hopes and plans both of the Volkswagen factory and of its customers.

Civilian production at the plant was shut down on 3 September. The plant was not yet fully equipped for car production – it still did not have a press shop, for example – and Porsche was given the order to develop military vehicles from the basic Volkswagen design.

Porsche designed the first military Volkswagen with an elegant aerodynamic shape analogous to the civilian version. The body had a rounded form and was not dissimilar to that of today's beach buggy. But this did not meet with much enthusiasm from his military clients. A military vehicle was supposed to be angular and martial, not elegant. Although Porsche's second version of a jeep-type vehicle, the Kübelwagen, did look angular and military, it was considered too small. Porsche was to strike it lucky with his third design, prototype No. 82, which was completed in 1940 and which lived up to military expectations: it was angular and of the right proportions, it had a chassis with high ground clearance and special rear axle reduction gear to compensate for the absence of four-wheel drive, and it was easy to manoeuvre and light enough to be manhandled by its four-man crew on rough terrain.

With these military prerequisites met, the Volkswagen went into series production as Kübelwagen Type 82, of which 52,000 were built up to 1945. It proved successful in service on all fronts and was rated

4.8

4.9

so highly by the Allies that the British Eighth Army under Field Marshal Montgomery had the operating instructions translated into English when they continued to drive the Kübelwagens abandoned by German troops in North Africa.

From 1942 onwards another military version of the Volkswagen, known as the Schwimmwagen Type 166, went into series production. Its construction at Wolfsburg coincides with a dark period in the history of the factory, which was by now producing weapons as well as vehicles. Prisoners of war from the eastern front were forced to work in the factory.

The Schwimmwagen was an amphibious vehicle with four-wheel drive. Again Porsche had to alter the design in order to please the military. The original version, Type 128, was initially deemed too large and cumbersome and the dimensions were scaled down in order to arrive at a satisfactory result.

The vehicle had a closed hull underneath which, since the car was also intended to float in the water, was also to some extent hydro-dynamically shaped. In the water it was driven by a propeller, which was coupled to an extension of the crankshaft. This vehicle had a top speed of approximately 80 km/h on land, and with a speed of approximately 10 km/h in the water, was very manoeuvrable. This type was produced in very small quantities (just over 14,000), though it must be said that the overall production figure for all military versions of the Volkswagen was relatively small in view of the factory's daily capacity of 1,000 vehicles.

In terms of technology the militarised Volkswagens were decidedly advanced with their rear-mounted engines, their air cooling and in some cases their amphibious capability. From a stylistic point of view, however, they clearly resembled the vehicles of other countries' armed forces. They had simple, purpose-designed bodies with no particular stylistic attributes. They were cost-effective to manufacture and easy to repair.

The experience gained with these Volkswagens under extreme conditions on all fronts during the Second World War was to prove an important factor in the reliability of the postwar Volkswagen, and found its way into a host of design improvements which ultimately benefited the series production cars.

At the end of the war two thirds of the factory lay in ruins. The Americans, as the first Allied troops to enter the Wolfsburg area, were not greatly interested in the factory since in the long term it would lie outside their zone of occupation. When the British arrived in the summer of 1945 they were concerned at the impossibility of the 6,000 people employed at the Volkswagen plant finding alternative employment and feared increased nationalist or, more especially, communist agitation. Foreseeing the need to build vehicles for the occupying powers and ultimately also to meet the urgent transport needs of the civilian authorities, they immediately set about reorganising the plant.

Orders were given to assemble vehicles from existing parts. These were essentially Kübelwagens or standard Volkswagens on a Kübelwagen chassis. Only 57 ordinary Volkswagens were produced that year, but a start had been made and those keen to see the Volkswagen plant survive could see a glimmer of light at the end of the tunnel.

1. Reichsverband der Automobilindustrie, Unpublished report, 1936

4.10

Ferry Porsche, the 356 and the foundation of the Porsche marque, 1948-1956

by Michael Cotton

1998 marks the fiftieth anniversary of the production of the first Porsche car, the Type 356. The small Austrian village of Gmünd seems an unlikely setting for the birth of a motoring legend, for the sawmill in which the first 356 was made was situated 20 kilometres from the nearest railway station and the region had virtually no skilled labour. However, within two and a half years, Ferry Porsche built up a workforce of three hundred at Gmünd and produced no fewer than forty-six aluminium-bodied sports cars.

The prototype had the Volkswagen air-cooled engine in the mid-position, ahead of the rear wheels, but Ferry's father believed that the car would do better with its engine at the rear, as in the Volkswagen. Every subsequent 356 model was rear-engined and had room for two jump seats in the back and space for luggage. The mid-engined prototype weighed only 585 kg and although the 1,100 cc engine developed a mere 35 hp it was said to have impressive acceleration.

Every Porsche body was hand-beaten by a master craftsman from the old Austro-Daimler works in Vienna, Friedrich Weber, who joined the Porsche company in April 1948. He spent two months making the first streamlined body to the design of Ferry Porsche and Erwin Komenda. These cars were certainly the equal in quality and finish to anything being made by more sophisticated factories in the immediate postwar period.

Orders were flooding in from around Europe but Ferry Porsche anticipated a total market of only five hundred cars when he moved the company back to Stuttgart in the spring of 1950. Production of the 356 continued in a rented corner of the coach-builder Reutter's premises in Zuffenhausen. Here the body-shell was constructed of steel rather than aluminium. The five-hundredth Porsche 356 was built in March 1951 and demand was now almost overwhelming. By the time the model finally went out of production in 1965, the total had reached 78,000.

The origin of the Porsche 356 was the Volkswagen, but not the model we know as the Beetle. In 1939 Ferdinand Porsche and his team designed a sports version of the people's car for competition in the Berlin-Rome road rally, a race linking Hitler's Berlin to Mussolini's Rome. Using all the available stretches of autobahn, including the 600-km stretch from Berlin to Munich, this race would have required flat-out driving and a car with an aerodynamic body.

The Berlin-Rome car (Porsche Type 64) was ready for testing in the early summer, and three were built. The driver was seated in the centre of the car with an offset seat behind him for a notional passenger. The Volkswagen 1.1 litre engine developed only 40 hp but this was enough to give the Type 64 a top speed of 140 km/h. The planned race was cancelled when war broke out in September 1939 and the three Type 64s were stored. Only one of these forerunners of the Porsche 356 survives.

In the summer of 1944, when Stuttgart was under heavy bombardment, the Porsche family moved, together with their workforce and assets, to the safety of Gmünd. Ferdinand Porsche and his son were detained by the Allies when the war ended. Ferry was released after eleven months, in July 1946. His father was interned by the French at Dijon until August 1948 and had no part in the design of the 356. In his absence, Ferry Porsche and Karl Rabe, his father's chief designer, set about re-establishing the Porsche firm as a design consultancy and, for the first time, as a manufacturer.

In 1949 Ferry Porsche reached an agreement with Volkswagen's managing director Heinz Nordhoff that Porsche would become Volkswagen's design consultants, and would receive a royalty for each Volkswagen produced. Neither party could have anticipated then that

5.1

5.1
Type 356 chassis being carried to the Reutter coach works in Stuttgart, 1951.

5.2
The workshop in Gmünd where the first Type 356s were made.

5.2

5.3
The impressive engine of the
Cisitalia Grand Prix car.

5.4
The Porsche Type 64 Berlin-
Rome car dating from 1939.

the production figure would eventually exceed twenty million. In return, Volkswagen guaranteed Porsche all the parts he would need to continue production of the 356, and furthermore appointed the Porsche family to distribute Volkswagens in Austria. Ferry Porsche's elder sister, Louise Piëch, handled this side of the business.

Charles Faroux, who had been involved in negotiations to free Ferdinand Porsche from internment and was an organiser of the Le Mans 24-hour race, met Porsche again at the Paris Show in October 1950 and proposed that Porsche should send a team to Le Mans the following June. Porsche initially demurred, suspecting that strong anti-German feelings would be demonstrated, but later accepted Faroux's personal guarantee that the Porsche team would be well received. And so it was, but Porsche did not live long enough to see the car bearing his name compete in the race. Weakened by his internment, Ferdinand Porsche died on 30 January 1951, only a few months after the celebration of his seventy-fifth birthday.

Three cars, all aluminium coupés, were prepared for Le Mans, but luck was not on Porsche's side as two of them were written off before the race even started. One was badly damaged during a reconnaissance when a cyclist crossed the driver's path and forced him off the road, and the second was destroyed in a crash during practice.

The third, one of the two original 356.2 coupés, did take part in the event and distinguished itself in the hands of the French Porsche importer Auguste Veuillet and the driver Edmond Mouche. Despite the low power of the Porsche engine, no more than 44 hp, they reached speeds of just over 160 km/h on the long Mulsanne straight, finished in twentieth place overall and won the 1,100 cc class. It averaged 73.545 mph and its best lap was covered at 85 mph.

Porsche was now established as an international competitor. Throughout Europe, and even in America, the 356 was sought after as a fine sports car and as a potential competition model. The lightweight aluminium coupé, which was catalogued at 640 kg, was raced in the early 1950s but it urgently needed more power.

For sport customers, Porsche bored the flat-four engine in 1951, raised the capacity to 1,488 cc and further tuned it with two Solex downdraft carburettors. The power was almost doubled, to 70 hp, and the tuned 356 had a genuine top speed of 162 km/h. One such car was run flat-out at the Montlhéry banked circuit near Paris, setting new record average speeds of 159 km/h for 2,000 miles and 24 hours.

The debut of the Porsche 356 at Le Mans in 1951 marked the beginning of an almost unbroken run of appearances in the 24-hour race, and it was not long before major developments were being undertaken. The cars, usually with engines ahead of the rear wheels, were designed to take Porsche ever nearer to the top of the overall classification. The Type 550, for instance, claimed fourth, fifth and sixth places overall in 1955 and three years later its successor, the 718 RSK, went a little better in claiming third, fourth and fifth places overall.

The engines installed in the early lightweight 356 coupés were actually reduced in capacity, from 1,131 cc to 1,086 cc, in order to compete in the 1,100 cc category. Larger capacity engines followed, with 1,290 cc and 1,582 cc and in tubed-up S trim they developed 60 bhp and 75 bhp respectively. The first 356 Carrera model appeared in 1955 and its 1,498 cc engine, specially made with aluminium crankcase, pistons and cylinder heads, developed a very healthy 100 hp. With a kerb-weight of 950 kg this model was something to be reckoned with in competitions.

The name Carrera – Spanish for 'race' – was borrowed from the Carrera Pan Americana in Mexico which suited the Porsches well. Hans Herrmann won his class easily in 1954 and finished third overall in a

5.3

Type 550 Spyder, and subsequently 'Carrera' was used by Porsche to denote cars intended for racing.

It is true to say that there has never been a disappointing version of the Carrera, although the purists raised an eyebrow when it was applied to the 924 model which raced at Le Mans in 1980. The 356 Carrera GTs, and later the 911 Carreras, always promised the ultimate in road car performance. The original 356 Carrera GT went on sale in the autumn of 1955, and three years later a 1,600 cc version appeared with 115 bhp.

The 356 model could have been created for rallies too. In 1952 the Porsche marque completely dominated the most arduous marathon of all, the Liège-Rome-Liège rally, which was won by Helmut Polensky in a 1,500 cc lightweight coupé; Hans Herrmann was third and Paul von Guilleaume fourth. In fact five Porsches finished in the top ten positions and won the team prize, too; an achievement that caught the attention of the whole world.

The creation of the legend was now well underway, and the class victory at Le Mans whetted Ferry Porsche's appetite for greater success and wider publicity. He laid down a ground rule that would stand Porsche in good stead to this day.

'The question did come up as to whether or not racing, as an activity, was worth the cost to the maker. I believe the theory behind it is clear. Journalists' reports of races are far more effective and more convincing than most forms of advertising, and they cost little or nothing. Money thus freed from unnecessary advertising can be used to gain valuable racing experience, and the lessons so learned mean that next year's model can be a better car.'[1]

Porsche's philosophy was absolutely correct in those early days. The company worked on a maximum production basis and still could not meet customer demand. Porsche's customers were usually sports orientated, but they were not all sportsmen or sportswomen. King Farouk of Egypt owned an early model, as did Prince Bertil of Sweden. Prince Egon von Fürstenberg was another royal customer and industrialist Alfried Krupp bought a new Porsche every year. Madame Pompidou, wife of the French statesman, owned a 356 (and later a 911).

But what was the real attraction of the Porsche 356? What marked it out from its principal rivals, the Jaguar XK120, the Aston Martin DB2, the Frazer Nash, Allard J2, and the Ferraris which were, in Italy, rising to fame on the back of early Grand Prix successes? Unlike most of these cars the Porsche was styled for efficiency rather than for

5.5
Spyder racing cars under
construction, c.1954.

5.6
Porsche's racing manager,
Huschke von Hanstein, in the
first 550 Spyder, c.1954-1955.

showroom appeal: efficiency in terms of low aerodynamic drag, low weight, high straight line speed with relatively little power, and with good economy.

Denis Jenkinson was an early convert to Porsche when the 356 was introduced to the British market, covering more than a quarter of a million miles in ten years while *Motor Sport*'s Continental Correspondent. As such, he attended every Grand Prix in Europe for four decades, and most of the classic sports car races until the late 1960s.

'Right from the start', wrote Jenkinson, 'the Porsche 356 either appealed or offended, and there was no in-between. With the engine located at the rear, and very little wind noise, it was a remarkably quiet and relaxing car in which to travel long distances.'

'The welded steel body was unusual at the time for its complete lack of seams, the wings flowing into the body very smoothly. Its aerodynamics were very good, as shown by the fuel consumption which rarely dropped below 30 mpg, and its speed capabilities relative to its horsepower. It sat very low on the ground and its overall height was a mere fifty inches.'[2]

Like Volkswagens, though, the early Porsches were renowned for the sometimes anti-social rear engine characteristics: 'In those early days the 356 would corner at reasonable speeds without drama,' Jenkinson observed. 'But if you went a bit faster then the rear suspension would tend to let the wheels tuck in as weight transfer had the effect of raising the rear of the car, so that the swing axles dropped. This would instantly induce violent oversteer, which if not caught would result in a spin.

But the 356 had a sort of early warning system, called *wischening*. 'As you were nearing the cornering limit,' Jenkinson noted, 'the action of the rear axle would transmit itself through the gearbox mounting and then via the gear-change linkage, so that the gear-lever flapped violently and struck you on the knee. If you met a Porsche owner with a badly bruised knee you knew that he had been driving pretty near the limit in his 356. The Porsche was that sort of car.'[3]

The Porsche badge was introduced late in 1952, incorporating the crest of the city of Stuttgart upon the shield of the region, Württemberg. Above this was a bar incorporating the Porsche name, the typeface already stylised in a way that is associated with the marque. It is a coincidence that the badges of both Porsche and Ferrari bear the Prancing Horse, but that is all it is: a coincidence that relates to Stuttgart, not to Porsche's aspirations to knock the Italians off their steed!

Porsche needed to develop the 356, but carefully, redesigning the Volkswagen elements to make them stronger, better, and to give them a unique identity. Not for a moment, though, would the key elements be changed: the 356 would always be powered by an air-cooled four-cylinder engine, would always have torsion bar suspension, and would always retain its fine build quality and inherent strength.

Development of the engine and gearbox proceeded quickly and thoroughly. After all, the four-speed crash gearbox that Ferdinand Porsche designed for the original Volkswagen was not good enough for the Porsche; as soon as the engine was tuned, or the weight of the car increased, the gearbox would break in hard use.

Porsche's own gearbox was introduced late in 1951 for the 1952 model year, much more robust and with Porsche's own patent split-ring synchromesh on all gears.

Engine development continued apace, taking on a distinct Porsche identity. The larger capacity 1300 S version was introduced for the 1953 model year, with 60 hp, featuring Hirth roller-bearing crankshafts. The importance of these had to be played down, not because there was anything wrong with them but because customers insisted

5.7

on having such an engine, and Hirth could not supply enough components. The following year Porsche specified their own roller-bearing crankshafts, and all the customers were happy.

Dr Ernst Fuhrmann, a young engineer working in the research and development department, was given responsibility for designing an advanced, powerful unit suitable for future racing activities. It was not to be a full race engine, though, rather it had to be suitable for installation in the higher performance road models.

This power unit, always referred to as the Fuhrmann engine, was highly complex (it took one skilled mechanic a week to strip down, overhaul and rebuild) with four gear-driven camshafts. Most of the materials were light alloy (for the individual, finned cylinder-barrels, heads and pistons), there were two spark plugs per cylinder and two Solex twin-choke carburettors were installed. The first version, with 1.5 litre capacity, developed 100 hp at 6,200 rpm, and was installed in the Type 550 road-race competition car first seen in 1954. Notably this returned to the original concept with the engine in the centre, behind the cockpit, as there was no need to compromise the design for passengers or luggage.

The 550's debut was on the Mille Miglia in 1954 when Hans Herrmann and Herbert Linge (the latter Porsche's test driver) finished sixth overall. Later, a batch was built for the road, even more powerful with 110 hp. Herbert von Karajan, the conductor, was an early customer. Another was James Dean, the actor, who gave the 550 model an undeserved notoriety after he lost his life in a road accident when driving one.

Books have been written about the continuous developments and successes of the Type 550 – in which Umberto Maglioli won the awesome Targa Florio outright in 1956, Porsche's first World Championship race victory – and its successor the Type 718, which brought increasing fame to Porsche and their customers. There was parallel development, no less intense, of the 356 model and its own derivatives, the Carrera and Abarth Grand Touring models for instance, which continued to astonish with their consistently high performances in races and rallies in every part of the world.

Volkswagen's engine was discontinued when the 356A model was introduced for the 1955 model year (from September 1954) as Porsche now made their own three-piece motor. This was an autumn of great significance as Porsche introduced the Speedster version (Type 540), initially for the American market, creating a considerable stir. The waistline was lowered by 35 mm and the windscreen was lowered and given a wrap-around profile, giving the Porsche a much sleeker look, more in keeping with the 356.001 prototype.

Ferry Porsche led his company's twenty-fifth birthday celebrations at Zuffenhausen in 1956, coinciding with the production of the ten thousandth 356. They were, of course, celebrating the official registration of the Porsche design consultancy in 1931 and although this was, and remains, a significant date, the anniversary which is more often celebrated today is that of the first car to bear Porsche's name, in 1948.

Notes
1 F. Porsche and J. Bentley, *We at Porsche*, New York, 1976.
2 Denis Jenkinson, *Porsche 356*, Osprey AutoHistory, London, 1980, p.22
3 ibid., p.30

Butzi Porsche's Masterpieces – the 911 and 904 Carrera GTS, 1962-1972

by Tobias Aichele

The Porsche 911 is universally recognised as the epitome of the Porsche sports car, whereas even today the Porsche 904 Carrera GTS is sometimes mistaken for a Ferrari. Despite their many differences, the two cars have one thing in common: they were both designed at more or less the same time by F. A. Porsche – a member of the third generation of the Porsche dynasty – and both have made history for the Porsche company.

These cars were developed at the beginning of the 1960s in response to a dual need within the Porsche company: firstly, it was vital to find a worthy successor to the 356; secondly, the Porsche production range had always included a car for motor sport enthusiasts which offered owners a real chance of winning in competitions. Here too, Porsche had a gap to fill. Since the era of the Spyder RS and RSK, only the Abarth-Carreras had managed to achieve success in international GT sport.

Ferry Porsche's eldest son, Ferdinand Alexander, known to everybody as Butzi, joined the firm straight after leaving the renowned Hochschule für Gestaltung in Ulm. He was initially assigned to vehicle body development under Erwin Komenda and soon showed a considerable talent for styling. So, although the young designer's suggestions were considered, it was Heinrich Klie who took overall charge of the emerging project to find a successor to the 356, together with the American designer Count Albert Goertz, who had risen to prominence as assistant to the design guru Raymond Loewy. Klie, a skilled pastry cook, set up the Porsche modelling department in 1951. Erwin Komenda, who had been responsible for sheet-metal engineering and design at

6.1
Porsche Type 911,
model year 1967.

6.2
Butzi Porsche working on
a plasticine model of the
Type 911, 1961.

6.2

6.1

6.3

Porsche since 1931, had designed various experimental cars at the beginning of the 1950s which were intended to form a successor to the 356. For Komenda, there was no difference between the technical and stylistic aspects of body design, and he would consequently not tolerate any designer looking over his shoulder. So although some overall trends were discernible when Butzi Porsche started work on the successor to the 356, he had virtually complete artistic freedom in designing the later 904 GT car.

In the meantime the need for a successor to the 356 was becoming more urgent, although the problem had not yet been clearly defined. The older generation at Porsche clung to the notion that they could build a four-seater fastback. 'I always said that it wasn't true a Porsche could only be a Porsche if it had a fastback,' recalls Butzi Porsche. 'I also took the view that the two requirements, to design a four-seater car with a fastback, were incompatible. But my father always wanted a fastback in order to emphasise the relationship with the 356.'[1] This is how Butzi Porsche explains the difference of opinion. Despite this controversy, Butzi Porsche embarked on an initial interpretation of the new car on 28 August 1959 as Type 754 T7. In the choice of wheelbase he was guided by the two Type 530 experimental cars designed by Komenda which were in turn based on the Type 356. For these, 2,400 mm was taken as being the minimum for a four-seater. The 356 series had a wheelbase of 2,100 mm. Butzi Porsche quickly set about producing a plasticine model on a scale of 1:7.5. 'Although I sketched my ideas out roughly in order to check the overall lines, I then very quickly transferred everything to the model, since I could always picture the forms quite clearly,' says Porsche.[2] The young designer consistently used plasticine as a modelling medium, whereas Heinrich Klie still worked with clay, which had to be kept wet when shaping it.

The first plasticine model was finished on 9 October 1959, and a modified version just six weeks later. This version was then made up in cast resin and painted blue. Fortunately the study met with great approval, as work had already begun on a full-scale mock-up.

The model on a scale of 1:7.5 was so exact that plans were drawn up from this, on the basis of which modelling then proceeded. The 1:1 T7 was created on a wooden frame fitted with Type 356 axles.

6.3
Butzi Porsche with the Type 911,
1968.

6.4
Porsche Type 911 Targa,
model year 1969.

This was necessary for manoeuvring purposes. The plasticine was applied by heating it to a temperature of fifty to sixty degrees centigrade in a pottery kiln and pressing it on to the base. To increase the stability of the material, nails were driven into the wooden frame, which were then modelled over.

The wooden frame was kept approximately 10 cm smaller than the proposed size. The thickness of plasticine was constantly checked with templates, which were applied very precisely using a vernier height gauge. The intervals for application of the templates were predetermined on the drawings. The first task of the modellers was to apply sufficient plasticine, and then, together with the designer, shape the model in strict accordance with the design drawing. They scraped away with home-made tools. Butzi Porsche initially used coarse saw blades, 'since one did not get to the form quite so quickly when smoothing off,' he says.[3]

The first 1:1 scale plasticine mock-up was completed on 28 December 1959. The front end of the car was virtually in its final form. The low body also had the characteristic, flowing wing contours which reminded observers of the 356. The prominent, slightly inclined main headlights immediately proclaimed it a Porsche. 'For us, even then, the main headlights were a major aspect of the design,' recalls Butzi Porsche.[4] The large areas of glass were altogether untypical of a Porsche and in direct comparison made the windows of the 356 look like peepholes or gun ports. The rear was strongly reminiscent of Pininfarina studies of the time, an impression emphasised by the enormous rear screen. The overall line of the rear sloped very gently down but had a slight step, which meant that normal-sized adults in the rear passenger seats tended to catch their head on the rear screen. The rear seats were arranged as in the 356, that is with two bucket seats with backrests that could be folded forwards to accommodate more luggage. Butzi Porsche accepted the restricted seat height for rear passengers, because under no circumstances was the T7 to acquire a hump. It had to fulfil his father's demand for a fastback.

At the end of 1959 Ferry Porsche finally gave formal approval for the design and development of a new Porsche model. He also gave orders that no Porsche feature from the 356 era was to be adopted unquestioningly. Another decisive step towards the 911 came when Ferry Porsche announced that he was in favour of a smaller, sportier car. The wheelbase was to be 2,200 mm. Ferry Porsche insisted upon a fastback, while his son Butzi explained that a much more elegant four-seater could be achieved simply by means of a slightly stepped rear end. Erwin Komenda supported both the fastback and the four-

6.4

seater solution. Finally, after Goertz's proposal had been deemed much too American, it was decided that Butzi Porsche would pursue the project under the designation Type 644 T8, as would Erwin Komenda under the designation Type 754 T9.

Thus, two rival camps developed. Komenda paid scarcely any attention to Ferry Porsche's stipulations because he held too strongly to his vision of a four-seater fastback. Under his direction three full-scale wood and sheet metal mock-ups were produced by 31 January 1962. The bumper unit, however, was much too bulky and the indicator lights looked as if they had been stuck on as an afterthought. Above all the Komenda designs became bigger and heavier. 'The T9 looked bloated,' recalls Butzi Porsche.[5] Ferry Porsche decided on an unusual step in order to ensure that the model designed by the styling section could not be modified in the hands of the car body designers. He approached Walter Beierbach, then managing director of the coach-builders Reutter, and had his son's model sketched and translated into engineering drawings.

In 1961 Butzi Porsche was appointed head of the modelling department, causing Heinrich Klie's demotion by a rank. At the same time the engineers Theo Bauer and Werner Trenkler joined the model-ling department, so that suggestions could not only be represented but could also be translated into drawings. Butzi Porsche wanted to prevent the design and experimental sections from discarding at the outset suggestions that they felt were unfeasible.

Under the designation Type 644 T8 the development work was finally focused in a single direction. Work began on the design of a two-seater with a 2,100 mm wheelbase and a rear fuel tank. The first plasticine model on a scale of 1:7.5 was completed in December 1961. In the meantime, however, the designers had come up with a very compact front axle, which even allowed protected positioning of the fuel tank. For this reason the idea of a pure two-seater was quickly abandoned and another 100 mm were added to the wheelbase again, resulting in a successful fastback car with 2+2 seats, the subsequent 911. Butzi Porsche says, 'I was utterly convinced: the body will be great!'[6] He was to be proved right.

The fibreglass body of the 904 Carrera GTS, the design of which originates from the same period, also proved a great success. Butzi Porsche drew the sleek form freehand and received valuable support in implementing it from Gerhard Schröder, one of his best designers.

6.5
Porsche Type 904 Carrera
at Sebring, 1964.

6.6
Three Type 904s at Sebring,
1965.

6.7
Porsche Type 911 Carrera, 1973.

6.7

In February 1963 when the successor to the 356, which was christened the 901 (later 911), was well into the development process, the full-scale model for the body of the Porsche 904 was sent to the aircraft manufacturer Heinkel in Speyer. Because lightness was a priority in this car, the Porsche designers decided to cooperate with an aircraft specialist who had experience with synthetic materials. The model for the 904 series, which can be imagined as a polished wooden block, represented the positive form from which negative moulds were made. These moulds were first sprayed with a separating lacquer so that, after curing, the fibreglass parts could be easily removed. A wall thickness of 2 mm was specified for the 904, so that three layers of glass fibre had to be applied.

In November 1963 Heinkel delivered the first finished body to Porsche. The result was impressive. Two men could comfortably carry the body which weighed only 100 kg. The box section frame weighed another 50 kg. Without fuel (110 litres) the 904 weighed only 650 kg, which with the 180 hp four-cylinder Carrera engine gave it a top speed of just under 270 km/h. Between 1964 and 1966 Porsche built 116 of these cars, slightly more than the 100 vehicles required for homologation, including eight examples with the new flat six-cylinder engine, which was developed for the 911, and two two-litre prototypes developing 230 hp from eight cylinders.

The costs both of developing the 904 and of producing a replacement for the 356 imposed a heavy financial strain on Porsche. The cost of the 901 alone ultimately reached DM 15 million by the time the new model was ready for series production. No official figure was given for the cost of the 904. In any event Porsche's financial resources were so drained that in 1963 Porsche withdrew from all Grand Prix events. Porsche couldn't afford a flop with the new car because of the large financial investment.

Having had to forego demonstrations throughout the whole of 1963, and with customers unable to drive the 901 at the International Motor Show, the sales department organised a demonstration programme in Germany and elsewhere in Europe. Sales executives Dieter Lenz and Hans Klink were to demonstrate the cars to all dealers, in order to allow potential customers a chance actually to experience the cars. It was difficult for the sales personnel at the International Motor Show to understand why the 901 was to cost DM 7,000 more than the 356. In the meantime the sales manager, Wolfgang Raether, had succeeded in getting the price reduced by DM 1,500 by the time the first cars were delivered.

It is clear from an internal memo dated 9 December 1963 that three versions of the 901 were planned: firstly a 901 deluxe, as shown in Frankfurt with full leather trim, costing DM 22,400; secondly, a standard version with four-cylinder engine and imitation leather trim, without chromium plating on the wheels and with a wooden steering wheel, costing DM 17,500; and thirdly, a 901 'S' with a 150 hp engine, costing DM 23,900. As only the first version was ready for delivery by the end of 1964, only this one was offered on the sales tour.

At a development meeting on 25 August 1964 Hans Tomala stated that the design work on the new Type 901 car was virtually complete. But it would still be a long time before the 901 could be filed away, because a more attractively priced version with a four-cylinder engine, a version with a sliding roof, a competition car with lighter body parts and above all an open-top version were still on the cards.

At the beginning of October 1964 Porsche exhibited the 901 at the Paris Motor Show and announced the forthcoming delivery of the first cars. At this point Peugeot suddenly became aware of the new sports car, and in particular its designation. Because Peugeot had given all its cars a three-figure designation with a zero in the middle since 1929, the French insisted on this copyright and sought to enforce trademark protection. Legally, however, these claims were applicable only in France. In order to be able to carry the same designation for the new sports car all over the world and because France was an important export market, the designation was changed without further ado to 911. Internally, however, and particularly on the drawings and in spare parts numbers, the designation 901 was retained for a long time in order to avoid inconsistencies. The same procedure was followed with the 912 four-cylinder model, still to be unveiled, which was originally called the 902. The racing prototype 904, on the other hand, retained its designation. Responsibility for this goes to the racing manager Huschke von Hanstein who argued that Porsche had already been marketing the 904 for a year without Peugeot's raising objections. Subsequent competition models also had a zero in the middle.

The first series production cars were delivered at a sales conference in Stuttgart on 27 October 1964, while the modelling and design departments were stepping up their work on an open-top 901. The first internal presentation of the mock-up of this car to the special developments section of the body shop took place on 12 June 1964. Those present included Ferry Porsche; his son Butzi; Hans Tomala, technical manager; Walter Beierbach, managing director of Reutter; Harald Wagner, domestic sales executive; Erwin Komenda, head of bodywork design; and Fritz Blaschka, design engineer, who took the minutes. Wagner pleaded for a full convertible without rollover bar, but even he recognised that too many expensive modifications, such as a lower profile windscreen and modification of the rear-end shape, would have been necessary. So at this meeting they finally agreed on the solution with a fixed bar. Ferry Porsche, however, still wanted a few modifications: for example he stipulated that the front roof retainer be designed as narrow as possible in order to improve entrance to the vehicle and make it more like a convertible. Furthermore the rear edge of the rollover bar was to be further modified and the folding hoops originally proposed were to be omitted in order to increase the head-room above the occasional seat. All modifications were to be implemented as quickly as possible on the existing mock-up which was made of aluminium sheet cladding on a timber base.

The press release prepared for the Frankfurt Motor Show in September 1965 described the latest Porsche model, the Targa, as neither a convertible nor a coupé, neither a hardtop nor a saloon, but something altogether new. It could also boast that the Targa was the first series production car in the world to incorporate a safety or rollover bar. It was the star attraction at Frankfurt. The new Porsche attracted enormous publicity and even the federal President had Ferry Porsche explain to him the thinking behind the safety bar.

Technical hold-ups meant that delivery of series production cars, scheduled to begin in spring 1966, had to be deferred until 23 January 1967. By then, however, three versions of the Targa were available: the 911 (130 hp), the 911S (160 hp) and the 912 (90 hp).

With the 911 and the 911 Targa, as well as the 904 Carrera GTS, Butzi Porsche succeeded magnificently. In engineering terms the 904, with its fibreglass body, anticipated much that later became commonplace in racing car construction: mixed steel/synthetic construction, low weight and small front face. It became one of the most successful racing cars of the 1960s and is still considered one of the best-looking.

The shape of the 911 is still captivating today. With this car Butzi Porsche probably had the biggest hit in motoring history; at any rate the 911 became the epitome of the German sports car. However, Butzi Porsche is less satisfied with the current version, the Carrera, bearing the internal designation 996. 'The current model is too trendy,' says Porsche. 'For me the 911 remained eternally young, simply because of its characteristic shape and reduction to an absolute functional minimum. The new model, on the other hand, represents a break with this principle, at any rate in the refined fittings and the shape of the headlights which, to me, are incomprehensible.'[7] 911 purists will, no doubt, agree with Porsche. Nevertheless, one thing is sure: the new 911 will also be a success. It is just meant for a new generation of customers.

Translated by Michael Bettney

Notes
1-7 F.A. Porsche in a telephone conversation with the author

6.8

Ferdinand Piëch and the development of the 917, 1968-1972

by Andrew Frankel

It is one of the greatest ironies in motor-racing history that the Porsche 917, a car which developed into the most powerful ever to race and which held the record for the fastest lap of any circuit in the world by any car in the world, was born out of an attempt by the motor sport authorities to slow sports cars down.

It was in the middle of 1967 that the then governing body of motor-racing, the CSI, announced that, for the following season, sports prototypes would have their engine capacities limited to just three litres. The effect of this edict was to throw sports-car racing into disarray. There was, however, a loophole in the rules. In an attempt to bring less highly specialised, more accessible sports cars to the track, manufacturers were allowed to race with engine capacities of up to five litres as long as fifty vehicles were produced, a figure so high that no manufacturer of pure prototypes would be able to build enough to homologate them for these new Group 4 regulations.

The problem was that no one else could either. Lola, for example, had just commissioned its T70 programme complete with 5.7-litre engines and had no hope at all of being able to produce fifty five-litre cars. Happily, the authorities relented and reduced the number of cars needed to be produced to twenty-five before one could race in Group 4. It would allow the smaller teams to race without running the risk of the major manufacturers homologating a prototype under the rules. Or so they thought. Ferdinand Piëch, the middle son of Ferdinand Porsche's daughter Louise, thought otherwise. Piëch, continuing the tradition of close involvement in the family company, had joined Porsche in 1963. By 1965 he was appointed head of research and in 1968 was promoted to head of development. In great secrecy, he prepared a single new car and submitted it to the CSI complete with enough parts to make a further twenty-four. When this was rejected, Piëch simply had the parts made into cars and there could be no further argument. The Porsche 917 was born. It complied with every regulation in the book and there was nothing the dismayed CSI could do to stop it racing.

To say it caught the sports car world unawares is an almost insulting understatement. The first time it ever ran in public, at the Le Mans test day in April 1969, it circulated the track three full seconds a lap quicker than anything else despite being entirely undeveloped and not yet even homologated. By the time the practice for the race proper came around, the gap between the 917 and the next fastest car had doubled. In its first ever race, at Spa-Francorchamps, it beat the Ferraris, Fords and Lolas to pole position.

What, then, did the 917 have that the others lacked? Compared to the true prototypes, running to the three-litre formula, the answer was obvious. Its engine, at 4.5 litres, was not only 50 per cent bigger, it also produced, from day one, at least 560 bhp, compared to the 360 bhp of the most powerful three-litre Porsche 908. In its own class, its power advantage over the opposition was still probably 100 bhp but with this came a kerb-weight of just 800 kg, compared to an average Group 4 girth of not much less than a tonne. Even when Ferrari responded to the challenge in 1970, the result, the beautiful 512S, weighed 880 kg and possessed just 550 bhp (by which time the 917 had moved on to 580 bhp) despite an engine with the full five litres, four valves per cylinder. Moreover it lacked the power-sapping air impeller fan upon which the Porsche relied for its cooling.

Porsche achieved these extraordinary statistics not simply through incredible technical ability but also through unrivalled attention to detail and a surprising amount of pragmatism. The reason, for instance, that the 917 did not use the full engine capacity allowance at first was that, fundamentally, the flat-twelve, 4.5-litre motor was the

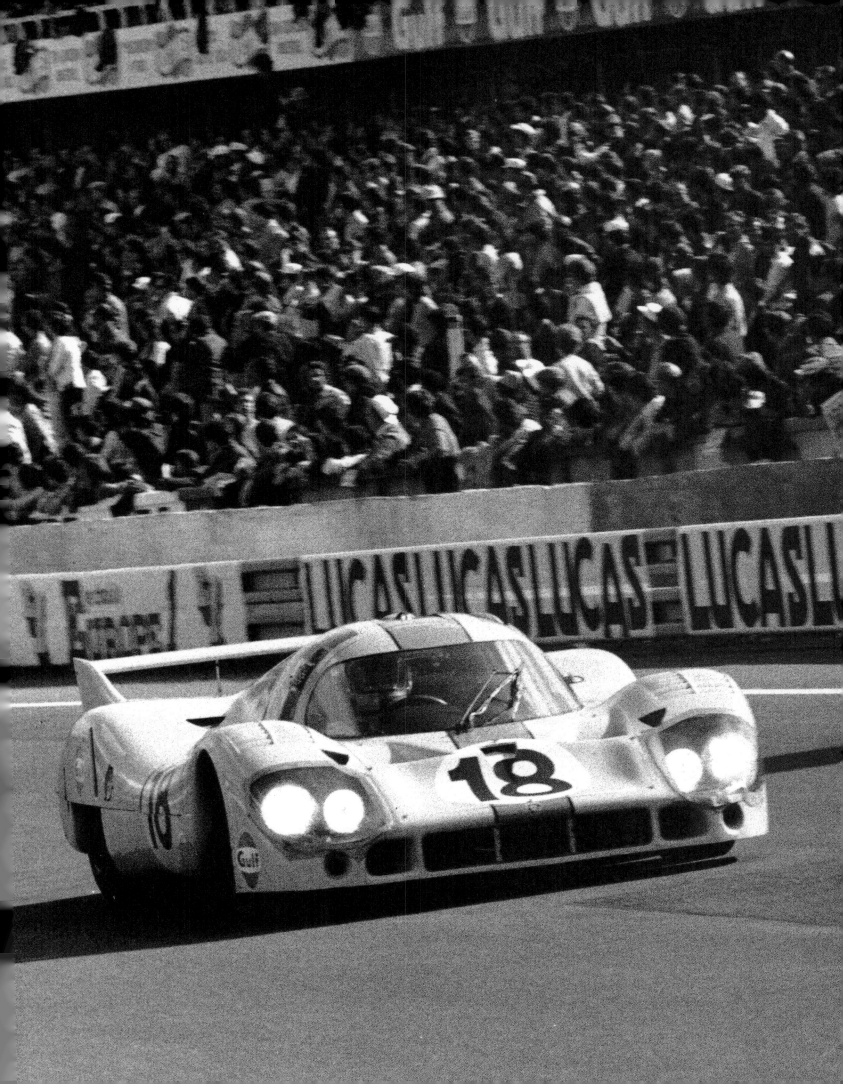

flat-eight, three-litre motor with another four cylinders added on, enabling Porsche to use a vast amount of internal components already tried and trusted in the 908.

The trick with this engine (and where it differed from the 908) was for the power to be taken from its centre, not from the end as in a conventional power plant. This allowed, in effect, two short crankshafts to be used, so avoiding the torsional vibration which would have been inherent in a single crankshaft of twice the length. Not only did this mean the engine would be more reliable, it could also rev higher and produce more power.

Nor was innovation kept solely under the bonnet. The 917 used glass-fibre bodywork with an outer skin just 1.2 mm thick which, in its entirety, complete with the windscreen, seats, wings and even the wiring loom, weighed just 95 kg. Extensive use of magnesium and titanium throughout the rest of the car made sure the running gear set similarly slimline standards.

It is tempting, therefore, to think the 917 was a complete success from the first day it poked its nose beyond the gates of Porsche's experimental department. The truth was rather different. No one doubted the potential of the 917 and the performance of which it should have been capable. Simple maths showed that it produced 700 bhp for every tonne of weight, compared to around 625 bhp per tonne for the best of the opposition. What maths failed to show, though, was that all the power in the world is no good if it can't be used and, in those early days, the 917 showed a disturbing lack of road-holding. Jo Siffert, one of the bravest of all and the man who put it on pole for its first race at Spa, wouldn't drive it in the race itself, preferring a slower but somewhat more stable 908. To this day Richard Attwood, who would win Porsche's first Le Mans in a 917 the following year, remembers only too vividly driving down the straight at over 200 mph, looking in the mirror and seeing the horizon lowering as the back of the car started to leave the ground. To this day he describes the 1969 917 as the worst racing car he ever drove.

7.2

7.3

7.1
A Type 917 at Le Mans, 1971.

7.2
Ferdinand Piëch at the Targa Florio, 1967.

7.3
917 Short Tail at Daytona, 1971.

7.4
The unveiling of the Type 917 at the Geneva Motor Show in 1969.

7.5
A Type 908 at the Targa Florio, 1970.

7.4

It is therefore perhaps surprising to learn that Attwood rates the 917 that followed it as the best racer he drove. After the end of the 1969 season Porsche and JW Automotive, John Wyer's formidable Slough-based team which had been appointed to run the works cars in 1970 and 1971, substantially shortened the rear bodywork and, at a stroke, solved the fundamental aerodynamic problem with which the 917 had been born. It never looked back.

In the following season its dominance was so complete that it won seven out of the eight world championship races it contested, including both 24-hour races at Daytona and Le Mans. The same number of victories were to come its way in 1971 giving Porsche the championship for the third year in succession. Throughout both seasons, just four races did not fall into Stuttgart's hands, with Ferrari winning at Sebring in 1970 and Alfa Romeo claiming the spoils at the Targa Florio, Brands Hatch and Watkins Glen in 1971.

This did not happen without continual development of the car. The engine capacity increased to 4.9 litres and then, for 1971, to the full five litres allowed by the regulations which, combined with greatly reduced internal friction courtesy of Nikasil cylinder-liners, pushed its output over 600 bhp. Acting in conjunction with further aerodynamic refinement, this meant the 917 could haul itself down the Mulsanne Straight at Le Mans at speeds in excess of 240 mph.

It was all too much for the authorities. They stated that, for 1972, all sports cars would not only be subjected to a three-litre capacity but also a minimum weight of 650 kg. The 908, which had mopped up so effectively at the Nürburgring and on the Targa Florio in 1970, weighed fully 100 kg less than this limit. Faced with an ineligible 917 and a 908 with the key to its speed removed, Porsche withdrew from the championship, leaving an open season, at last, for Ferrari.

For the 917, however, a new chapter was about to open up in North America. Here CanAm racing had been, for some years, resounding to the thunder of huge American V8 engines, unrestricted in size or power output. At the time of Porsche's arrival on the scene,

7.6
On the set of Steve McQueen's film *Le Mans*, 1971.

7.7
Ferdinand Piëch (right) with Jo Siffert at Sebring, 1968.

7.8
Type 917, 1970.

McLaren represented the state of the art with its 800 bhp, eight-litre M8. Clearly something extra was needed for the 917. That something extra was called a turbocharger.

The result was the Porsche 917/10. All worries about matching the power of the McLarens disappeared as its output rose towards and, finally into, four figures. Ominously for the opposition, Porsche had not even been trying for maximum power, preferring to concentrate on making sure the dreaded throttle lag, that affects all turbo engines to one extent or another, was reduced as far as possible. And just as Porsche had teamed up with John Wyer for the sports car championship, so it did with Roger Penske for the North American series. The driver was to be the brilliant Mark Donohue, winner of the Indianapolis 500, but when an accident put him out for almost the entire 1972 season, George Follmer stepped into his seat and steered the 917 to yet another championship.

Donohue was back for 1973 and Porsche provided him with what would prove to be the ultimate 917 weapon. Called the 917/30, its engine was stretched once more to 5.4 litres, its power output upped to 1,100 bhp. It still weighed the same 800 kg as the first 917 had in 1969, but now it had almost exactly twice the power. Putting two 1998 Formula One engines under the bonnet of a small family hatchback would not produce a higher power to weight ratio.

Donohue and the 917/30 arrived after the first two races of the 1973 season (both won by the 917/10) and from that moment no one else even counted. They won every one of the remaining races that season. Once more the officials found themselves faced with allowing the indomitable 917 to continue its steam-rolling of the opposition or acting to stop it. Predictably it was the latter course they chose, drafting regulations for the 1974 season which militated so much against the use of turbochargers that Porsche was forced to withdraw. The 917 seemed finally to have had its day.

But just as the 917 had been created by rules designed to stop such a car being built, so those rules designed to kill it killed only the competition they had been designed to protect. By the end of 1974 there was such little interest in CanAm racing the series was scrapped.

The 917, on the other hand, was not yet done. Although now prevented from racing in any major series on the planet because it was too quick, there was one last little bit of business for the 917 to conduct, just in case anyone still had the slightest doubt that it was the quickest racing car the world had ever seen. With the redoubtable Donohue at the wheel, one of only two 917/30s ever built took to the Talladega SuperSpeedway in Alabama in 1975 to try and lap a race track faster than any other car in history. His average speed over an entire lap was 221.1 mph. It would be years before another went so fast.

Usually racing cars are retired because, over time, the competition catches up and a new model is needed. The 917 never looked likely to suffer such an indignity. It signed off its tour of duty just as it had started, simply miles ahead of anything else.

Note
1 *Motor Sport*, London, September 1997

7.8

Porsche: new directions
1972-1998

by Hilton Holloway

Had Porsche's new model strategy, carefully developed in the 1970s, worked out, production of the 911 would have ended in the autumn of 1980. It would have been an impressive life. During the sixteen-year production run no changes were made to the design of the body shell and the only aesthetic changes were due to mandatory American-market 'impact' bumpers. The continuous and impressive incremental improvements to the relatively crude suspension and old-fashioned air-cooled engine would have been an ample tribute to the engineering genius of Porsche, even if some in the company were embarrassed by the age of the vehicle on which the genius was being lavished.

But the 911 was reprieved. The decision was taken at the same point that Porsche announced that its chief executive, Professor Dr Ernst Fuhrmann, would be replaced after eight years with the company. Fuhrmann's master plan for Porsche's future was to base the model range around more modern, front-engined, rear-drive sports cars powered by conventional, water-cooled engines.

Fuhrmann believed that the 911, hampered by the rear-engined mechanical layout shared with the pre-war Beetle and fatally flawed by the air-cooled engine, could not live long into the 1980s. It might be tricky to get the flat-six engine through future exhaust emission and noise pollution standards. Despite Ferry Porsche's discontent with the complete break from the design direction laid down by his father, the new model range sought to bury the 911 as a viable product.

However, by 1980 Fuhrmann's strategy was clearly failing to fulfil its promise. The 911 was outselling the 928 by almost two to one and 911 production was running at double the number required to break even. Despite healthy sales, the 1976-launched 924 was beginning to fade as the decade turned and the 928, launched in 1978, was selling at only half the planned production rate, according to sources at the time.[1]

Perhaps convinced that his instincts were right all along, Ferry Porsche found a replacement in Peter Schutz, a German-born, American engineering graduate said to have been close to Porsche's own philosophy of reviving the 911 and expanding Porsche's research and development facilities in order to market the company's engineering skills. Schutz took over on 1 January 1980.

Schutz and Porsche would, over the next fifteen years or so, have reason to be grateful for the existence of the front-engined range, but perhaps most of all for the excellence of Tony Lapine's in-house styling studio. Porsche had already demonstrated its ability to carry out a first-class engineering job and then further refine and develop the idea to a level that completely belied the starting point.

Lapine's styling abilities mirrored this perfectly. The 924's early 1970s styling was extremely far-sighted in avoiding the vogue for brutally hard-edged wedge shapes so perfectly represented by the Triumph TR7. Lapine's 924 benefited from a languid elegance and restraint that included futuristic details such as the integrated bumper assemblies and absence of front window quarter-lights. A complete avoidance of period passions ensured a very long life for the 924's basic design.

The 944, ultimate realisation of Fuhrmann's strategy, was unveiled in 1981. By then Schutz had already given the go-ahead for a fresh round of 911 development work and was quoted as saying, 'My view is that nothing will replace the 911. It's a pure-bred sports car and for people who like its nature there is really nothing else. It is guaranteed a future brighter than ever before.'[2] Schutz must, though, have had cause to be grateful for the arrival of the 944 which may at first have simply looked like a handy stop-gap until the 911 model-line was revitalised in stages.

The 944 was perhaps Porsche's first project which showed that the styling and engineering philosophies were capable of remarkable

8.1

8.2

8.1
Porsche 911 GT1, road
version, 1996.

8.2
Porsche 911 Carrera, 1997.

feats of improvement and development. Based on the basic skeleton of the 924, the most important new component in the car was the engine, a Porsche-designed, 163 bhp, 2.5-litre, balancer shaft-equipped, four-cylinder unit cleverly created from half of the 928's V8.

Ultimately, Porsche power meant the 944 was regarded as a 'real' Porsche by both the press and marque enthusiasts. Modifications to the suspension and transmission mountings, an upgrading of the brakes, a rejig of the interior and attention to detail that even extended to the layout and fixing of under-bonnet components ensured the 944 was a completely different market proposition from the 924. Furhmann's new model strategy finally paid off.

However, even the considerable engineering development might not have been enough to make the 944 fully convincing had it not been allied to Lapine's masterful restyling. In effect the 924's central section simply received new, wider wings front and back, as well as integrated bumpers. The result was remarkable. The tiptoe appearance of the 924 was eliminated and replaced with a much more powerful stance. The 944's look was achieved by flaring the wings over the wheels and Lapine's stylists handled the resulting surface forms with a superb deftness.

'Blistered' arches are usually crudely grown out of a car's body-work. Lapine's handling of the rear arch's surface form – its sharp edge developed from the shoulder of the door skin – allows the shape to be defined by pools of shadow or highlights depending on lighting conditions. Even better is the complex interchange of surfaces on the top of the front wings and the instinctive chamfered trailing edge of the front wheel arch – both ample demonstrations of Porsche's timeless styling sensitivity.

Despite Schutz's assurances of longevity for the 911, there was still a strong feeling that the 911's days were numbered, especially with the arrival of the excellent 944. The car's aged quirkiness did not sit well at the beginning of a decade that was already promising significant technological advances for family cars.

8.3
Porsche 911 Targa, model year 1996.

8.4
Porsche 924 Carrera GT, 1980

8.3

Even accounting for Schutz's insistence on a bright future for the 911, and the developmental abilities of Porsche demonstrated by the 944, no commentator could have predicted the extraordinarily prescient leap into the future that was the 959. The car was unveiled just over two and a half years into Schutz's reign, at the Frankfurt show in September 1983 as the *Gruppe B* design study. Though strictly designed for entry into the new Group B rally competition class (necessitating plans for a 200-car production run) practically every technical feature and advancement of the 959 eventually found its way into the mainstream 911. Indeed, the forward thinking packaged in the 959 was directly responsible for keeping the 911 concept alive for well over a decade and its influence was even felt by the 911's ultimate replacement.

Like the 944, the 959 was based on the standard skeleton of the 911 shell, fitted with a completely new nose and tail and wings made from Kevlar. The floor pan had to be substantially modified because Porsche abandoned the ancient chassis and adopted electronically height-adjustable, wishbone-type suspension on all four corners, a highly advanced four-wheel drive transmission (using a computerised anti-slip device which varied the torque being fed to each wheel, depending on the road conditions) and a six-speed gearbox.

Although based on the standard flat-six, the 959's engine developed 400 bhp from just 2.85 litres, thanks to the twin-turbochargers' meticulous design that included polished titanium connecting rods. Though the engine's cylinders were air-cooled in Porsche's traditional manner, the new four-valve cylinder-heads were water-cooled.

If the technology spoke of the next decade, the styling reached into the new millennium. Although the original *Gruppe B* model was rather stiff and lacked the subtle surface treatment of the 944, the factory pictures of the production 959 just two months later showed a very different article. Porsche's stylists handled the extra ten inches of width extremely well, particularly in the connection of the front and rear wings with a skilfully-handled massive sill section.

The headlamps which leant backwards under flush covers with less prominent wing tops seemed to break one of the basic rules of 911 identification, though the new nose was still readily identifiable. Even the two organically sculpted air intakes in the upper rear wing, seemingly at odds with the tension of the 959's rear end, blended into the overall design. The 959's tail treatment, with the hooped wing stretching over a new full-width tail lamp graphic, was also particularly effective. All this proved that the 911's character did not revolve around a continuing facsimile of the original 1963 design. After the 959 there were no doubts about the potential longevity of the 911. Indeed, Porsche patented the 959's body shape.

Despite the improvements to the 924/4 series (the highly modified and highly regarded 944 Turbo and a 924 with the 944's Porsche engine – known as the S – both launched in 1985) and the dogged sales performance of the 911, Porsche experienced a serious sales collapse from 1987, particularly in the US and British markets. Between 1986 and 1987 the cost of the UK 911 Carrera rose from £25,000 to £31,000. Predictably sales slumped in Britain by a quarter in 1987.

Worse were the results from America, at that time Porsche's largest market, where sales collapsed by more than half between 1987 and 1988. Porsche had benefited from seven prosperous years, and blamed the slump on a weak dollar, the aftermath of the stock market crash ('Black Monday') and stronger competition. Critics said the company had been better at amassing record profits than establishing a long-term product strategy. By the end of 1987 Peter Schutz had been asked to resign.

Heinz Branitzki, installed as chairman on 1 January 1988, revealed 'the discussion about an entry-level Porsche is over ... it is financially impossible ... a Porsche for beginners is a used Porsche.' Branitzki aimed to take the brand back upmarket.[3]

Porsche's two major influences over design direction also changed in 1988 when engineering chief Helmuth Bott retired and was replaced by Ulrich Bez and styling boss Lapine was replaced by Harm Lagaay. Lagaay and Bez had recently worked together on the clever BMW Z1 roadster. Porsche's perilous position in the late 1980s was underlined by two statistics. The 944 still accounted for more than 50 per cent of production and the three-model range was ageing, the youngest at eleven years, the oldest twenty-six.

Some commentators suggested that Porsche's once-invincible image of well-engineered good taste had been damaged by the end of the 1980s, especially in Britain. The 'yuppy' effect put sizeable numbers of 911s on the roads, especially in the capital city, often funded by high earnings in the financial sector. The red 911 became a clichéd symbol of the often-parodied 'loadsamoney' attitude that was said to mark the boom years of the Thatcher government.

Peter Schutz's assertion in 1980 that the 911 had a bright future was finally realised with the launch of the 964 series – still under the 911 designation – in late 1988. Eighty-five per cent of the components were new. It also looked much crisper and more modern. Porsche had retained the old 911's central section, doors, bonnet and front wings, but designed new wraparound bumpers, resculpted the rear wings and fitted a 959-type rear light strip. As with the styling of the 959, the visual success of the 964 could be attributed to the skill in surface treatment of the new exterior panels, in particular the effective 'cleaning-up' of the old 911's fussy sill covers, rain gutters and impact-resistant bumpers. The crass 'tea-tray' spoiler of the outgoing 911 was replaced by a retractable spoiler which emerged from the engine lid when the car was travelling above 50 mph.

Development of the 964 had begun in early 1984, a few months after the 959 was unveiled, so it wasn't surprising that the first version of the 964 to go on sale was the four-wheel drive Carrera 4. Under the fresher skin lay a new floor, modified to incorporate the four-wheel drive system and a heavily modified engine (up from 3.1 litres and 235 bhp to 3.6 litres and 250 bhp).

Most importantly the suspension was redesigned, with the torsion bar system – which can be traced through the 356 back to the prewar Volkswagen – scrapped in favour of a more modern design. The near-flush underpan of the 964 and other subtle aerodynamic tweaks

8.6

8.5
Porsche 968 Coupé, 1992.

8.6
911 Construction at the Porsche factory, 1981.

8.7
Porsche 959 *Gruppe B*, 1983.

8.8
Chassis and engine of the Porsche 911 Carrera 4, 1988

8.5

8.7

8.8

brought the car's drag co-efficient down from 0.395 to a very respectable 0.32 – excellent for such an ancient silhouette. The 964 Carrera 2 (two-wheel drive) followed a year later.

While the 964 was another textbook example of Porsche's theme of radicalism and refinement, this approach was countered by the launch of a concept car at the 1989 Frankfurt Show. The Panamericana was developed by chief stylist Harm Lagaay. Based on the Carrera 4 chassis, the Panamericana aimed to take the 911's familiar silhouette into the 1990s by developing a modern interpretation for the most recognisable elements of the design (the proud wings and headlamps, the wraparound glass house, flared rear arches and sloping engine deck).

Despite the boldness of the approach – including the strong graphic of the nose-cone indicators and engine vents and tail lights – the car was poorly received. The heavily-blistered body sides and semi-exposed wheels were most criticised. However, Lagaay's use of the flowing line of the 911's cockpit top as an all-round roll-bar for the fabric Targa roof was an inspired piece of developmental thinking.

Perhaps it was this fundamental rejection of the radical development of the 911 aesthetic that led Porsche to start its most ambitious project ever. News of the 989 began to leak out in early 1990, shortly after the arrival of new chairman Arno Bohn. It would have replaced both the 944 and 928 in 1994. In a reverse of the Panamericana approach, the styling was a refinement while the engineering concept was radically new.

The 989 was a remarkable concept, and undoubtedly the ultimate realisation of Porsche's developmental approach. It wrapped the next-generation styling of the 911 over an update of the 928's front-mounted V8 engine layout. The newest element was the capacity

8.9
Grant Larson, design sketch
for the Boxster, c.1991-1992

8.10
Porsche 968 CS, model year
1994.

8.9

.10

for five passengers and a hatchbacked boot. The 989 was to have been very expensive and to have sold at a rate of around 12,000 each year. The styling was remarkable – a near-perfect transcription of the 911 into a much larger executive car.

When the project started Porsche was enjoying a financial revival, partly thanks to the new-generation 911. By early 1992, however, the company's fortunes had taken a serious dip and money had been lost on an ill-fated attempt to enter Formula One racing. So serious was the position that it was rumoured that the Porsche and Piëch families would be forced to sell out to a large manufacturer. In 1992 the company sold just over 4000 cars in the all-important US market: in 1986 it had sold over 28,000. 'The next years will be very difficult,'[4] said Bohn at the time. So difficult, in fact that the 989 project, after a very significant investment, was cancelled during 1992.

In 1993 Lagaay said of the 989, 'Everybody thought it could never be a sports car, but we proved that no matter where the engine is, no matter how many seats the car has, no matter what the concept is, you can make a four-door sports car that looks like a Porsche.'[5]

Porsche's only new model during the recession of the early 1990s was the 968. Launched in late 1991, the 968 was the final development of the 924/944 range, powered by a three-litre, 240 bhp version of that original 928-derived engine. Lagaay's facelift of the 944 echoed the step-forward of Lapine's redesign of the 924. It was just as brilliantly integrated, if nothing like as fresh and original. New wings – with 928-style headlamps – met at a new front bumper marked by a prominent indicator and fog lamp cluster.

The 944's rear wings were carried over to the 968, but were now underpinned by a bold bumper/rear-panel moulding containing new red monotone rear lights. The bold split line between the bumper and the rear wings was cleverly exploited as a strong graphic element in its own right. Porsche's attention to production detail included a well-considered styling of the engine's cam cover and inlet manifolds.

While neither the 964-series 911 nor the 968 managed to reverse radically the corporate sales slide, the turning point of Porsche's fortunes – both in terms of design and financial health – can be traced to the Detroit Motor Show in January 1993. It was there that Porsche showed its second concept, the Boxster, a name derived from the boxer engine and roadster. Styled under Lagaay's guidance, the Boxster was a simple, mid-engined, two-seater sports car which, although based on established Porsche engineering, was a complete aesthetic break from the past, even if it was recognisably from the Porsche stable.

Lagaay had abandoned the languid lines and subtle surface tensions of the 928, 968 and 911, replacing them with a much busier, more dramatic approach. This policy was most marked inside where the interior was a riot of competitive curves and wildly-varying radii. It was also replete with applied detailing – or 'jewellery' as it was known amongst automotive designers. This included a tortoiseshell-type material, aluminium and brightly-coloured leather, as well as semi-functional details such as the exposed gear linkage and three-bladed fans mounted behind mesh in the air vent apertures.

According to Lagaay, 'The interior is totally different from any existing Porsche – the only thing that's the same is the five round dials in the fascia – and it demonstrates that quite an evolution is possible without losing our identity.'[6] Porsche, while planning to base its future model range around a mid-engined two-seater and an evolution of the 911, was clearly taken aback by the rapturous reception that greeted the Boxster's styling. So the decision was taken shortly after Detroit to bring the concept into production as far as was possible. Senior

8.11

8.11
Interior of the Porsche 944,
1981.

8.12
Panamericana prototype, 1989.

Porsche engineers visited the largest of its hard-pressed US dealers with the news. The dealers immediately began to distribute Boxster brochures and take firm orders.

Ironically, less than a year after the Boxster was shown, Porsche put the most heavily-modified and final development of the 911 into production. There is little doubt that the 993-series was Porsche's most comprehensively successful exercise in developmental styling and engineering. With the 993, Lagaay's team had taken the 911 aesthetic – exactly thirty years old – and moved it forward with enormous skill and subtlety. It had a strong claim to be the best-styled 911 of the whole line.

Although the inner structure was mostly unchanged, every exterior panel apart from the roof was either modified or replaced completely. Bravest of the changes was the switch to semi-reclined headlamps, first mooted in 1983 on the 959, mounted on wings that are both lower than those of previous models and flared behind the front wheel. The bonnet was also raised, giving the 993 a much smoother, more integrated nose. Modifications to the doors were hard to spot.

The rear wings became much broader in order to accommodate the new and highly complex sub-frame-mounted rear suspension (originally developed for the five-door 989) and filled out to merge almost seamlessly with the new rear bumper. Even the classic arrangement of the grilled engine cover was new: it sat higher, no longer following the downward curve of the rear window.

These comprehensive changes did not affect the interior which, aside from some minor rearranging of the switchgear and new seats, remained resolutely related to the original design, despite the often criticised ergonomics of the layout. The 993 also gained another 22 bhp (up to 272) in standard form, a new six-speed transmission and uprated brakes. The car was highly praised for its newfound civility and extremely sure-footed handling.

The 993-series also saw one of Porsche's cleverest design solutions, reintroducing the 911's side-window design 'signature' to the Targa roof model. The 993 Targa used a glass roof panel, the curve of which echoed that of the rear window, allowing it to slide backwards under the rear window. This solution meant the roof and side windows – the 911's sacrosanct areas – were replaced with beautiful and powerful 'flying buttresses' growing from the top of the rear wing and curving over on to the windscreen surround.

The 911 design development reached its peak in March 1995 with the 993 Turbo, a 400 bhp, four-wheel drive, twin-turbocharged coupé. Finally, the full influence of the 959 was seen on a series production car. The Turbo was an astoundingly fast and dynamic car that combined the modernity of unmatched cross-country ability with the idiosyncrasy and distinctive engine note of a thirty-three year-old concept.

The following year the flagship of the company's 1970s dash for modernity was killed off. The Porsche 928 survived eighteen years with minimal design and styling tweaks (the most notable being the replacement of the recessed rear lights with flush-fitting clusters). By 1996 the 928 still looked extremely fresh and individual (particularly the styling of the combined door and B-pillar and the boldness of the bumper-less body) and still more modern than the majority of cars born that year. Lapine's 928 was undoubtedly one of the best-styled (and engineered) cars of the twentieth century.

Three and a half years after its Detroit debut, the production Boxster – project 986 – appeared. It was the first all-new Porsche for nineteen years and received something of a mixed reception mainly because the dramatic proportions and much of the show car's detailing hadn't made it into reality. It had grown, gained a longer nose (necessary for crash protection) and generally lacked the surface tension of the concept. The sculptural sill-height air intakes were also lost and replaced with an innocuous intake in the leading edge of the rear wing. Even so, it was clear that the Boxster was another extremely well-executed styling exercise, again demonstrating that it was its subtle surfacing that set the company apart.

Negative reaction to the interior was rather stronger, as it had lost nearly all the show-car detailing. The overall design had also rejected Porsche's long-standing commitment to lean and disciplined volumes in favour of an ill-coordinated assembly of sweeping curves and ovoids. The oval theme of the central console spoke more of Far Eastern styling than restrained Porsche design.

But there was no doubting the quality of the Boxster's engineering and the car's road abilities were enthusiastically received. Based on an entirely new chassis and suspension (the front section of which would be shared with the new 911), the 2.5-litre, flat-six engine was now cooled by water for reasons of emissions and noise control. Yet its distinctive timbre remained.

One year later the 996 was launched, marking the end of the thirty-four-year reign of the original 911. The only parts shared between the 993 and 996 make up the rear suspension. Otherwise, the 996 was a clean-sheet design, though it shares its headlamps and some of the interior switchgear with the Boxster. It too has a water-cooled, flat-six engine.

8.12

8.13 and 8.14
The Boxster, 1996.

The 996 is longer and wider than the old car but succeeds superbly in capturing the essence of the original 911's design progression. The rear half of the 996 is exceptionally well developed. The rear lights, now much taller, sit on the corners of the tail. The rear bumper is deeper and the engine grille is now body-coloured. This gives the new rear end a greater authority and weight. Also cleverly handled is the side window graphic and even the swept-back windscreen fails to take away from the authentic look.

However, the wider cabin means the front wings, rear wings and doors form a continuous surface; the interesting conflict of the flared wings and inset doors has gone. So too has the alert look of the front end, as the wings don't protrude so markedly over the bonnet. The 996's headlamps are closer together than on the Boxster adding to the rather formless, pinched look of the new nose.

Both cars are engineered to exceptional standards of build and longevity, especially the chassis and power train. Porsche's achievements over the years have often been considered in terms of styling and performance. But for such a small, independent company to achieve such high-quality engineering (perhaps only occasionally bettered by one or two giant firms) is as, if not more, remarkable.

Porsche knows its future still lies with the 911 concept. The company's research and development boss at the time of the 996 launch, Horst Marchart (who has worked on the car since the original 901), says the next 911 in 2010 will again be a 'two-plus-two seater, rear-engined and powered by a flat-six'.[7]

Porsche's numerous diversions into fresh design possibilities have only served to prove what Ferry Porsche asserted in 1993: 'We can modify the 911, hone and improve it, but we must never alter either its character or its unmistakable appearance.' Porsche's unrivalled ability to develop continuously long-lived mechanical and styling concepts will ensure that that is the case.[8]

The essence of the 911 – that it is a compact two-plus-two supercar, highly engineered and built to the best mass-production standards – has yet to be effectively rivalled. To date, other 'supercars' have been either less wieldy, less well engineered or both. And no other automobile can challenge the 911's extraordinarily effective thirty-five-year design progression.

Notes
1 George Kacher, personal communication
2 *Car*, London, December 1981, p.54
3 *Car*, London, December 1988, p.121
4 *Car*, London, February 1992, p. 22
5 *Car*, London, April 1993, p.43
6 ibid.
7 *Car*, London, October 1997, p.76
8 *Car*, London, November 1993, p.97

8.13

Paul Frère

Paul Frère trained in Brussels as an engineer and began his career as a racing driver in the 1940s. His many achievements include winning his class at Le Mans in 1958 in a Porsche car and, in 1960, winning the South African Grand Prix and Le Mans outright. He has been writing as long as he has been racing and his book *The 911 Story*, which is now in its sixth edition, is generally regarded as the authoritative work on the subject.

Dr Michel Kaltschmid

Dr Kaltschmid was a founder of the Society for Austrian Motor History and editor of the Society's magazine *Austro Classic* between 1990 and 1995. From 1988 until 1991 he was the public relations manager for Jaguar in Austria. Since 1960 he has written on automotive subjects for *Die Presse* (Motor), *Auto-Revue*, *Austro Motor* and numerous journals. He is the head of a printing and publishing house in Vienna.

Karl Ludvigsen

Karl Ludvigsen is the author of *Excellence was Expected*, widely regarded as the definitive history of the Porsche marque. He has written more than twenty books and scores of articles on all aspects of motoring history. He runs a consultancy bureau to the motoring industry and is an executive of General Motors, Fiat and Ford.

Doug Nye

Doug Nye is a regular contributor to the *Daily Telegraph*, *Motor Sport* and *Classic and Sports Car*, and is the author of more than fifty books on all aspects of automotive history. He is a consultant to Brooks auctioneers and is one of the founders and organisers of the Goodwood Festival of Speed.

Dr Bernd Wiersch

Dr Wiersch has been Director of the Stiftung AutoMuseum Volkswagen in Wolfsburg, Germany, since 1983. He is also the archivist of Volkswagen AG and the author of numerous works on the history of the Volkswagen, Kübelwagen and Schwimmwagen.

Michael Cotton

Michael Cotton was editor of *Motoring News* from 1967 to 1976 and press and public relations manager of Porsche Cars Great Britain Limited from 1976 until 1983. He currently writes for the *Daily Telegraph*, *Motoring News* and *911 and Porsche World*. He is the author of a number of books on Porsche and has revised and edited Julius Weitmann's authoritative *Porsche Story*.

Tobias Aichele

Tobias Aichele is the author of *All about the Porsche 911*, *All about Porsche* and *Porsche 911 – Forever Young*. From 1993 to 1996 he was Porsche's chief press officer in Stuttgart. He now runs an independent press agency.

Hilton Holloway

Hilton Holloway studied industrial and automotive design and worked as a bicycle designer at Gary Fisher Mountain Bikes in the USA. From 1991 until 1992 he was head of research and development at Muddy Fox Mountain Bikes. He has written for *Carweek* and was a researcher and production assistant for the Discovery Channel's *Driving Passions*. He is currently news editor of *Car* magazine.

Andrew Frankel

Andrew Frankel has contributed to numerous books, television programmes, and magazines around the world on the subject of motor-racing. He is currently editor of *Motor Sport* and contributes regularly to the *Sunday Times* and *Autocar*, for which he was previously road test editor.